THE
PRIVILEGED POOCH

Luxury TRAVEL WITH YOUR PET
IN SOUTHERN CALIFORNIA

To:
Nathan,
Michele,

Happy Travels!

Maggie Espinosa

Marcel

Acknowledgement

Maggie Espinosa truly appreciates the assistance of all the businesses that provided information and photos for this book. She is grateful to her husband for tending to the home front while she was traveling, and offers special thanks to the original privileged pooch, Marcel, her fellow road warrior.

Cover and interior design: Carlsson Creative, 2010
Front Cover Photo: iStock Images, 2010
Author Photo: Craig Jones, 2010
Maps: Map Resources, 2010
Photos throughout book: iStock Photo 2010, Fotolia 2010

Library of Congress Control Number: 2010904092
Printed in the United States of America - Streeter Printing
ISBN: 978-0-615-35035-6

Table of Contents

San Diego 6

Palm Springs 48

Orange County

Dana Point/Laguna Beach 68

Newport Beach/Costa Mesa/Huntington Beach 88

Los Angeles

Long Beach/Palos Verdes/Marina Del Rey 110

Santa Monica 126

Beverly Hills 145

West Hollywood 161

Pasadena 179

Santa Barbara/Ojai 186

Introduction

According to the American Pet Products Association, approximately 45.6 million households in the United States own dogs. Of those homes, 21 percent travel with their canine. An increase in pup pampering has fueled the travel industry to embrace these scruffy scions. Pooch parents no longer must compromise their blissful luxury resort vacations in order to accommodate the hound. Hip Four and Five Star hotels roll out the red carpet for Fido, offering toys, beds, bowls, spa treatments, and pup-sitting services. Amenities aren't limited to hotels. Elegant alfresco restaurants, tourist activities, urban parks, and seaside beaches also welcome four-legged friends.

Southern California's luxury resorts mimic the region's laid-back attitude. They run the gamut from opulent to discreet. Neither is better than the other, they just play out differently. All have good taste and fine service. The 69 hotels in this book have been personally tested and approved by me and my Bichon Frise sidekick, Marcel. I've rated them on pet-friendliness using a "wags" key located on page 5. Some are more restrictive than others. If a resort's pet regulations are too stringent with weight limit, access in the hotel or exorbitant fees, I didn't include them in the book.

The same credo goes for my 55 restaurant recommendations. If management requires pups to be tied outside the patio, I don't consider them a pet-friendly establishment. I've only included the ones that allow dogs to accompany owners on the patio. Pets are never permitted inside. Keep in mind, the California Health Department changes rules frequently, which may affect the status of eateries suggested in this guide. The websites provided throughout the book are an invaluable tool in researching your desired destination further for any policy changes.

Only one of the 56 activities listed has a weight restriction; it's difficult to get a Bull Mastiff into a GOCAR. But the remainder welcome all creatures great and small. And the 38 shops mentioned give carte blanche to privileged pooches. Wags are not included with the bistros, outings or boutiques as they all permit pets with no stipulations.

A few accessories are imperative when traveling with pets. Most hotels require vaccination records confirming up-to-date inoculations. Take along any medications. While bowls are usually provided, it's smart to pack one, just in case. Eco-disposable sugar cane pet bowls or nylon collapsible bowls are convenient. Make sure to take plenty of drinking water and your dog's usual kibble, in case the hotel's pet menu fare disagrees with his sensitive stomach. Deviating from a pet's usual diet can have drastic consequences. A collar, leash, and waste bags are mandatory. Your pet's ID tag should be imprinted with your cell phone number in case the dog wanders while traveling. Last but not least, pack your dog's manners. Barkers, chewers, and growlers will be more comfortable at home.

When making reservations, inform the hotel that a pet will be accompanying you, and ask the fee and weight limit. Often, pooches are permitted to stay in the room alone, but it's not recommended. Being separated from owners in a strange location can lead to all sorts of "nasties." I've included an emergency veterinary hospital for each city, listed at the end of the correlating chapter.

So go ahead, explore, sniff, just nose around. My suggestions are only a springboard to the magnificent sights sunny Southern California has to offer you and your furry friend.

Each hotel is rated with "wags," which represents their level of pet friendliness. Four wags offer the most pet amenities, and one wag offers the least.

One Wag 🐾 = Pooches Permitted
Two Wags 🐾🐾 = Pooches Playground
Three Wags 🐾🐾🐾 = Pooches Pampered
Four Wags 🐾🐾🐾🐾 = Pooches Paradise

HOTEL PRICES:

$ = $90 to $150
$$ = $151 to $300
$$$ = $301 to $450
$$$$ = $451 and above

RESTAURANT PRICES:

Price per person for main course at dinner
$ = $1 to $14
$$ = $15 to $19
$$$ = $20 to $25
$$$$ = $25 and above

ACTIVITY PRICES:

$ = $1 to $15
$$ = $16 to $30
$$$ = $31 to $49
$$$$ = $50 and above

It's no surprise that this sun-drenched metropolis has been dubbed "America's Finest City." Perfect weather, miles of shoreline, award-winning restaurants, top-tier hotels and boundless activities are only a portion of its offerings. The spirited coastal community was voted "America's Best City for Dogs" by Dog Fancy magazine due to its Fido-friendly beaches, alfresco dining, and the most pet-inclusive environment in the Southland. From atop La Jolla's Soledad Mountain and Cabrillo National Monument to the Pacific's edge on Coronado Island and the San Diego Harbor, there is something for every two and four-legged vacationer.

SAN DIEGO

Sheraton Carlsbad Resort and Spa

The Grand Del Mar

Sheraton La Jolla Hotel

Tower23

Manchester Grand Hyatt

Omni San Diego Hotel

The W Hotel San Diego

Hotel Solamar

Loews Coronado Bay Resort

Sheraton Suites San Diego at Symphony Hall

Rancho Valencia Resort and Spa

The Keating

The US Grant

The Sofia Hotel

The Westin Gaslamp Quarter

San Diego Marriott Hotel and Marina

Warner Springs

Alpine

Oceanside
Carlsbad
San Marcos
Escondido
Encinitas
Solana Beach
Del Mar
Rancho Santa Fe
La Jolla
Pacific Beach
Julian
San Diego
Coronado

MEXICO

Stay

THE GRAND DEL MAR

5300 Grand Del Mar Court, San Diego, CA 92130 🐕🐕🐕🐕

(888) 314-2030 • (858) 314-2000 • www.TheGrandDelMar.com ($$$$)

....

Ascend to the pantheon of ultra-luxe resorts with a visit to this Five Star hotel. The Grand Del Mar blends sophisticated style with a relaxed atmosphere, resulting in a fresh interpretation of luxury. An average building cost of $1 million per guest room proves that mediocrity does not exist at this meticulous property.

The 249 rooms elicit wows, even from the unimpressionable well traveled. Miles of polished marble, a private balcony, and a bottom-less tub embody good taste on a co-lossal scale. Twice-daily housekeeping service keeps it spic-and-span. Certain rooms are designed for the approximately 5% of guests who bring a dog. A weight limit of 25 pounds and $100 per stay pet-

fee is hotel policy. Pet sitting/walking is offered through bonded and licensed Marion's Childcare. Grandmotherly love is showered upon pooches in the form of treats, numerous walks, and snuggles. The four-hour minimum allows enough time to unwind at The Spa, a definite must for all.

The Spa's 21,000-square-feet of calm graciousness is sure to confiscate aches and pains. Each treatment is designed only for The Grand Del Mar. Not to be missed is the 90-minute Renaissance body ritual. A soft-pack water cocoon cradles bliss-seekers as slathered mineral mud detoxifies the body. The spa's one-of-a-kind nuances such as framed vintage-style Hermes scarves along the corridors is just one of the reasons the elegant hotel is on top of all those World's Best lists.

The Addison Restaurant is another reason for the accolades. The AAA Five Diamond and Mobil Five Star beauty is named after the turn-of-the-century architect, Addison Mizner, who inspired the resort's design. Baby-faced Chef William Bradley has been at the

helm since its inception in 2006. His savory sea scallops practically levitate diners with their smooth, buttery taste. Their wine service is second to none.

An 8 a.m. guided walk through 4,000-acre Los Penasquitos Canyon Reserve will burn off Chef Bradley's dinner. Naturalist, Dylan Jones, welcomes two and four-legged adventurers on the four-mile jaunt.

Guests with lazier hounds bring a doggie backpack so furry friends can bum a ride when they tire. Jones' spiel is laced with humor and fun facts. Trekkers pass 140 years of stratum, cross an old stagecoach route, and identify unique flora such as the Chalk Dudleya, which lives up to 150 years — yet another exceptional experience while staying at this grand resort.

LOEWS CORONADO BAY RESORT
4000 Loews Coronado Bay Road, Coronado, CA 92118 🐕🐕🐕🐕
(800) 815-6397 • (619) 424-4000 • www.loewshotels.com ($$)
....

Loews is the proverbial poster child for pet-friendly hotels and is rumored to be the catalyst for the canine craze at upscale establishments. With only 18 properties in the U.S. and Canada, owner John Tisch has time to hone customer service, translating into alpha dog amenities for two and four-legged guests.

The hotel, splayed on a 15-acre private peninsula, has 439 rooms in five separate wings. Pooches of any size are permitted in any room, with only a $25 cleaning fee. A "Loews Loves Pets" welcome letter familiarizes guests with the resources, such as pet-sitting, a "Did You Forget" service providing forgotten leashes and collars, and a "Do Not Disturb" sign that lets housekeeping know a dog is in the room. Food bowls, treats, and biodegradable poop bags are standard.

Loews "Su'ruff Camp" exemplifies their VIP (Very Important Pet) attitude. The one-night package includes dog surfing lessons from Coronado Surfing Academy at picturesque Coronado Dog Beach a few miles from the hotel. Also included are board shorts or bandana for Bowser, a copy of "The Dog's Guide To Surfing" and a surf 'n' turf canine supper. Star students can "hang ten" in the hotel's annual surf dog competition held every June.

While Loews offers pets and people numerous ways to test-drive the SoCal lifestyle, ranging from sunset tours on a 27-foot sailboat to Capri speed boat charters, none is as unique as cruising the nearby canals in a gondola. Enjoy a one-hour ride at dusk through the Coronado Cays, where the average home costs $2 million. Italian music fills the air as young gondoliers sing an aria and passengers snack on complimentary hors d'oeuvres.

Catching waves and traversing the blue seas can tire out any pooch, so schedule a Mutt Massage. For $130 an hour, a Holistic Health Practitioner will come to the room and caress Fido's brachial, increase spine circulation through tail manipulation, and get legs and paws moving again using reflexology.

Pets are welcome on the Market Café patio, Cays Lounge patio, and Marina Terrace. For a special evening, hire a pet sitter and dine at Mistral. They serve locally caught seafood, and an array of veggies grown in the resorts private garden. No need to skedaddle back to the room, your hungry hound can have bow wow tenderloin or chow hound chicken delivered from the in-room menu.

RANCHO VALENCIA RESORT AND SPA
5921 Valencia Circle, Rancho Santa Fe, CA 92067 🐕🐕🐕🐕
(800) 548-3664 • (858) 756-1123 • www.ranchovalencia.com ($$$)
....

High standards are the norm at this veteran resort, which recently celebrated twenty years of excellence. Fashioned after a California hacienda, discreet luxury comes in the form of adobe casitas, hand-painted tiles, and clay-shingle roofs. Forty-nine villas dot the 40-acre property.

Bellmen stand at the entryway's circular driveway, shaded by a huge Zulu Fig tree. The resort cat, "Cassie," meanders close by, waiting for a treat and a pat on the head. Owners Mr. and Mrs. Collins, who live on the property, are animal lovers and can often be seen walking their two Yellow Labs. They charge $75 per day for pooches. A pet policy letter given at check-in summarizes dog-friendly areas, as well as the off-limit ones such as the pool, spa, and dining room.

The resort shares its exclusive zip code with high-brow residents Bill Gates and Madonna. The rural pocket of exceptionality is ideal for the calming and restorative hotel. Secluded suites with cream carpets, pillow laden sofas and warming fireplaces have French doors leading to a garden patio decorated with bougainvillea and citrus

trees. Special gifts await privileged pooches: a nylon portable water bowl, a tennis ball on a rope, and Greenie chew bones.

Unique art pieces including an Afghani Gypsy Grain Cart are sprinkled throughout restaurants and patios. Mother Nature's artistic talent can be viewed on the Sala Terrace as two and four-legged patrons snack on appetizers and sip fruity cocktails. The concierge will arrange a pet-sitter, allowing guests to dine at The Restaurant at Rancho Valencia, rated "one of the top ten in San Diego" by Zagat. Fido may have a meal prepared and delivered via room service.

The spa should be on guests' short-list. The playful terra cotta "clay bake" encourages amore as couples spread earthy goo on each other, soak in the sun, then splash away the mud in an outdoor shower. A more solitary venture is the Watsu — Japanese for floating in a warm-water pool while being massaged. Pooches are only allowed in The Spa Shop, but in-room treatments are available.

THE W HOTEL SAN DIEGO
421 West B Street, San Diego, CA 92101 ♥♥♥♥
(619) 231-8220 • www.whotels.com ($$)
....

W Hotel offers the best of both worlds – cosmopolitan chic in a beach town. Situated in the heart of the city, this 19-story, ultra-modern place resides in the ever-cool Gaslamp Quarter.

The "Pets Are Welcome" (PAW) program showers furry friends of any size with treats and toys upon arrival. A $100 non-refundable fee, plus $25 a night is charged. The usual amenities are in the room, as well as steps for small dogs to get up on their owners' bed.

Two-hundred-and-fifty-nine rooms are decorated in sea-blue and white to enhance the aquatic atmosphere. Pillow top mattresses and feather beds guarantee a good night's sleep. The obligatory Egyptian cotton sheets and large flat screen TV adorn each room. BLISS bath products and plush terry robes are top of the line. Rooms have catchy names, starting with the standard room, or Wonderful Room. Next is the Cool Corner Suite, then the Fantastic Suite and finally the Extreme WOW suite which goes for a few grand a night.

A hip, efficient, and pretty staff, or "talent" as they are called, keep the hotel hopping. The Whatever/Whenever concierge service ensures practically anything is a phone call away, catering to a guest's every whim 24 hours a day.

Visitors can dine at numerous hotel locations with their pup. Light fare in the lobby's Living Room bar and Magnet lounge includes sandwiches, salads and small plate tapas. Regional cuisine is served in the upscale signature bistro, Rice. Tasty treats include Peanut Butter and Jelly French Toast, Kobe Burgers with Maui Onions, and Blue-Cheese Spread.

A pooch-sitter is necessary for guests who want to kick back at the outdoor, rooftop bar, Beach. Visitors are invited to lounge by a fire pit while sipping martinis. Heated sand on Beach's floor keeps things cozy. A few steps away is Veranda Bar, which is a more intimate setting.

The Away Spa treatments are good enough to eat – the Spa-tini offers mani's, pedi's, massages, and martinis. While getting a treatment, healthy snacks such as fresh fruit or grilled shrimp salad are available, along with the not-so-healthy Angus burger. For the more serious spagoers, reflexology and massages are offered, as well as in-room treatments.

OMNI SAN DIEGO HOTEL
675 L Street, San Diego, CA 92101
(619) 231-6664 • www.omnihotels.com ($$$)
....

Baseball fans rejoice. Omni San Diego is the first U.S. hotel attached to a ballpark — the Padre's PETCO Park. Joe DiMaggio's cleats in the lobby are only a precursor to the Ty Cobb, Mickey Mantle, and Willie Mays treasures that await. Floors one, four, five, and six of the 32-story hotel pay homage to more baseball greats. Stop by the

concierge desk and pick up a complimentary memorabilia guide.

Stellar views come with each room, whether it's the San Diego Bay, burgeoning East Village, or the stadium. Mini-bars fittingly stock peanuts and Cracker Jack. True baseball devotees book rooms 1633, 1733, 1833, 1933, or 2033, as these overlook the field. To get closer to the action, a short walk across the fourth-floor skybridge deposits guests into the ballpark. A ticket is required to enter PETCO Park.

The Four Diamond Omni accommodates furry fans. Pets 40 pounds or less can partake in the "It's A Dog's Life" package, which includes a bed, a collar tag with the hotel's contact information, a list of dog-friendly locations and a complimentary "dog themed" movie. Yes, a movie. Pooches can choose from Lassie, Benji, or 101 Dalmatians. Advanced reservations are required and a $50 cleaning fee is added to the cost of the package.

A Fitness Center with all the bells and whistles is located on the Omni Hotel's sixth floor; pets are not permitted. But don't jettison a good workout because the dog is along on vacation. An in-room Get Fit Kit with dumbbells and stretch bands is offered at the front desk to use while on property. Also, the concierge has walking/jogging maps outlining the nearby two-mile promenade.

The outdoor heated pool on the sixth floor Palm Terrace and in-room spa treatments vie for the hotels most relaxing experience. The 8,000-square-foot patio pampers both people and pooches with extra wide chaises. The adjacent bar serves fruity drinks, brewskis, and light fare. Continued mollycoddling comes in the form of an Aloe Vera Massage or Day Breeze Deluxe Facial. There is no spa on the premises, so aestheticians make hotel-calls.

McCormick & Schmick's restaurant off the lobby serves the gamut, from huevos rancheros and buttermilk pancakes in the early A.M., to fresh seafood, steak, and salads in the late P.M.. The outside patio doles out lots of scrumptious treats for man's (and woman's) best friend.

THE KEATING
432 F Street, San Diego, CA 92101 🐕🐕🐕🐕
(619) 814-5700 • www.thekeating.com ($$)
....

Many hotels claim to be different, but this one truly is. The Keating is Italian sport car designer Pininfarina's first venture in the travel industry. They are best known for creating Maserati and Ferrari's sleek lines. Their edgy ideas have spilled over into a new level of cool in the hotel world.

The building's historic Romanesque-Revival brick exterior is contrary to the foyer's high-end haute. Eye-searing red walls backdrop the minimally furnished, compact space. Vases filled with huge an-

therium leaves flank the welcome desk, staffed by two Personal Concierge; "receptionist" is too generic for The Keating's lexicon.

Vacationers are escorted to one of the hotel's 35 stanzas (Italian for guest room), which is a vaulted space void of any interior walls. Pininfarina didn't want to disrupt the warm (bedroom) and wet (bathroom) zones. Furnishings are clean and linear. Materials of exotic woods add warmth to the utilitarian epoxy floors. A bedside Sanctuary (universal charging station) with eleven different chargers, and a LavAzza espresso machine meet the Keating's high techno-standards.

The in-crowd usually travel with their interminably adorable pooches, hence The Keating's 20-pounds-or-under Pet Ambassador Program. Fido's fee ranges from $50 for a one night stay, to $100 for two nights or longer. A crimson velvet dog bed adorned with gold tassels and Ferrari Red food bowls keep with la dolce vita motto. The Personal Concierge will walk dogs around the surrounding Gaslamp

Quarter if they're not busy.

Merk Italian bistro headlines Keating's uber-cool eateries. The subterranean restaurant located in the basement specializes in rustic dishes and wines from European vineyards. Adjoining nightclub Sway is a hot-spot for local VIPs and hotel guests. Those traveling with pets can have the Personal Concierge grab some take-out from the myriad nearby restaurants for you to eat in your room.

THE US GRANT
326 Broadway, San Diego, CA 92101 🐕🐕🐕🐕
(619) 744-2027 • www.luxurycollection.com/usgrant ($$)
....

This century-old downtown mainstay sits on land originally inhabited by the Kumeyaay Tribe of Indians, until they were persecuted and driven away by European denizens in the early 1800's. Acknowledging the injustice, in 1875 President Ulysses S. Grant passed an executive order allocating 640 acres in San Diego's East County for the tribe's new home.

Over the next hundred plus years, the vacated downtown terrain had numerous rebirths. Alanzo Horton's Horton House was built and prospered for 40 years, until Ulysses Grant Jr. demolished the property to make way for a luxury hotel in memory of his father. The next 90 years saw the hotel ebb and flow, with numerous attempts at ownership resulting in failure. This circuitous history lesson is imperative, because in 2003 the Kumeyaay Band of Indians came full circle with the purchase of The US Grant hotel and its land, returning possession to the original ancestors.

Today it stands as a true testament to patience and perseverance. A $56 million renovation showcasing marble columns, crystal chandeliers, and exotic woods has resulted in polished elegance. The Kumeyaay tribal flower, the primrose, is inconspicuously depicted throughout the hotel's eleven floors, whether it be on the lobby's $250,000 silk carpet, or diminutive statues perched among antique furnishings. Even though this notable building is a member of the Historic Hotels of America, they still allow well-behaved pets 35 pounds or less, and charge a $150 fee.

The bellman – or "social host" – gives details on restaurants, in-room spa services, and the fitness center on the way to the room. Information on dog parks, beaches, sitters, and pet-friendly restaurants is available at the concierge desk.

Each of the 270 guest rooms has a headboard painted by French artist Yves Clement. The ecru cotton canvas piece is fashioned in a Picasso-like style. Guests are welcome to purchase a headboard at the cost of $11,000. The bathroom is roomy and has a shower measuring eight feet by eight feet, with multiple spraying heads.

The Grant Grille and Lounge has been a hotel favorite since its inception in 1951. Old ways survive alongside the new, which is evident with the addition of martinis to the afternoon tea service. Pets are not permitted inside the restaurant, but the outside patio provides a great opportunity to people-watch. Twenty-four-hour dining is an in-room treat. Savor the hotel's specialty, Mock Turtle Soup, while Fido dines from German, Villeroy & Boch china on a silver tray.

SHERATON CARLSBAD RESORT & SPA
5480 Grand Pacific Drive, Carlsbad, CA 92008
(760) 827-2400 • www.sheratoncarlsbad.com ($$)
....

Guests young and old, two and four-legged, will love this 56-acre retreat located only three miles from the Pacific Ocean. Flanked by LEGOLAND theme park and The Crossings Golf Resort, a visitor's main conundrum is fitting in both activities.

Pooches are not only welcome here, the hotel indulges them with an "It's A Dog's Life" package which includes a chew toy, a pet-themed movie every night, the Sweet Sleeper dog bed, bowls, organic treats, and a Sheraton collar tag in case Rover roams. There is no pet fee,

and pet sitting and walking are available. The rules state no dogs over 80 pounds are welcome, but personnel has seen Great Danes stroll the property. The Pet Waiver says to keep dogs out of food and beverage areas, yet the patio of Twenty/20 restaurant has been known to host a fluffy Rubenesque pup or two.

The Ocean Pearl Spa is a Fido-free zone, with an expansive treatment repertoire comprised of facials, massages, and even a Little Lady manicure for girls 12 and under. Want to stick closer to the pooch? Schedule an in-room rub-down.

LEGOLAND has bestowed the LEGOLAND Bed & Brick Preferred Hotel moniker on Sheraton Carlsbad for its partnership with the park. Guests use their room keys to open a private gate entrance and purchase tickets at a small booth, sans waiting lines. Ideal for those traveling with younger kids…the two-legged kind.

SHERATON LA JOLLA HOTEL
3299 Holiday Court, La Jolla, CA 92037 🐕 🐕 🐕 🐕

(858) 453-5500 • www.sheraton.com/lajolla ($$)

....

Don't let the surrounding business district be a deterrent. This low-rise hotel is an eight- acre pocket of privacy complete with waterfalls and a Koi pond. As with any Starwood property, the Sheraton caters to pets and people equally. Weekends are more popular with families, as weekdays see an influx of business travelers.

Fido is welcome in any room, but must be attended at all times. An incidental $40 fee is tacked on the bill — well worth it, considering the pet amenities. At check-in, guests receive a bright yellow pouch depicting the hotel's trademark Golden Retriever puppy, which contains scented waste bags, plastic gloves, and hotel collar tag.

A navy blue dog bed branded with a hefty red "S," and food bowls are available.

The hushed corridors give no sign that canines accompany 7% of the hotel guests. Sporadic door hangers inscribed "My Best Friend's Here With Me" are the only clue. Perhaps the nearby three-and-five-mile walking route has tuckered them out. Guests unable to walk their pooches can ask the bellman to oblige, if he's not too busy.

The Butchart Garden-esque landscaping, with hundreds of palm trees and red begonias, is the perfect backdrop for lunch on Shooters Bar & Grille patio off the lobby. Here, diners get the fortification they need for an afternoon shopping spree at the adjoining La Jolla Square.

MANCHESTER GRAND HYATT
One Market Place, San Diego, CA 92101
(800) 233-1234 • (619) 232-1234
www.manchestergrand.hyatt.com ($$)
....

Southern California's largest waterfront hotel became pet-friendly after housing a menagerie of animals during the 2007 San Diego wildfires. The well-behaved predecessors opened doors for the inviting pet policy in place today.

Made up of two towers, Harbor and Seaport, the appropriately named Grand Hyatt boasts 1,625 rooms. The lobby, with its cathedral ceilings and soaring museum-like wall murals, is flanked by the respective towers. Everything is large: the chandeliers, the potted plants, the mosaics on the tile floor, everything.

Upon check-in, pets receive a blue plastic food bowl displaying the Hyatt logo, "The Daily Rover," artificial rolled newspaper, a privacy sign to hang on the door knob so housekeeping knows a dog is inside, and a welcome letter outlining nearby parks, beaches, and pet-sitting services. The Harbor Tower's tenth floor is devoted to animals and owners. The older of the two structures, it is slight on luxury, seeming in need of a remodel. The $30 a day pet fee is steep, considering. Policy allows one pet per room and it can not be left unattended.

Of the numerous resort eateries, four have alfresco dining. Ann-Marie's Coffee House has comfy patio chairs from which to sip lattes while gazing at stellar views of the marina. Pups are sure to get a tickle or two behind the ear from friendly patrons. A stones throw away is Sally's Seafood on the Water Restaurant. Stop in for the Jumbo Lump Blue Crab Cakes. Rounding out the selection is

Lael's and Redfield's. Although the 40th-floor Top of The Hyatt sky lounge doesn't allow dogs, it's worth the dollars to get a pet-sitter and head for the best view over the Pacific Ocean.

As with any hotel of this caliber, a spa, fitness center, and pool are *de rigueur*. Not taking themselves too seriously, the KIN Spa knows the way to truly relax is with a good drink, so guests can call ahead and have cocktails waiting to sip between their massage and pedicure. Call it a day on the fourth-floor pool deck, watching a theatrical sunset over the bay.

THE SOFIA HOTEL
150 West Broadway, San Diego, CA 92101 🐾🐾🐾🐾
(800) 826-0009 • (619) 234-9200 • www.thesofiahotel.com ($$)
....

A member of the Historic Hotels of America, this family-owned beauty is located on the periphery of San Diego's popular downtown Gaslamp Quarter. To qualify for HHA, affiliates must be located in a building at least 50 years old, and listed in the National Register of Historic Places. There are only 15 in California, four in San Diego.

Originally open in 1927 as the Pickwick Hotel, the Sofia's Neo-Gothic architecture stands out among nearby newer structures. The brick facade displays the original windows and wrought-iron fire escape. Inside, a complete remodel morphed the property into a unique fusion of history and modernity. Nuances such as wall scones with shades depicting historic hotel photos and a 24 hour business center in the lobby reflect this compatibility. Each of the 211 rooms has a pillow-top mattress, flat-screen TV, and new plumbing, ensuring excellent water pressure.

The Sofia's homeyness is conducive to guests and pets alike. The "Pampered Paws Package" welcomes pooches for a two-night stay in a deluxe suite. Food and water bowls, a pet pillow, and one-hour off-leash dog adventure to Fiesta Island beach are included. Make sure to specify the package when making reservations, as date and time need to be prearranged for your dog's escorted adventure.

For those who choose to forgo the package, there are "a la carte" stays. A one-time $50 pet fee will be charged. Bring bowls, as food paraphernalia is not provided. Fourth floor rooms are allocated for furry guests, who often convene in the hallway for introductory sniffs. Fetch Pet Care offers dog walks and in-room sitting. The front desk staff or concierge will make arrangements.

Current American Brasserie is the hotel's culinary superstar. Located on the ground floor's bustling Broadway Avenue, the streetside café is perfect to watch the world zoom by. The kitchen prepares

three squares from 6:30 a.m. to 10 p.m.. Menus change with the season, but the house beverage, Lavender Lemonade, remains constant. The wait-staff caters to pets with fresh bowls of H_2O and extra bread. Skittish dogs may not like the noisy city sounds.

A postprandial workout will be in order. The second floor 24 hour fitness center is just the place to stair-step off extra calories. The adjoining yoga studio has private and group lessons. No pets permitted in the exercise areas, but in-room spa services reunite visitors with pups.

SAN DIEGO MARRIOTT HOTEL & MARINA
333 West Harbor Drive, San Diego, CA 92101
(619) 234-1500 • (888) 236-2427 • www.marriott.com ($$)
....

The most pricey Marriott in San Diego is worth every penny.

Plopped in the heart of America's Finest City, the Four Star, water-front property has bragging rights for best location. A short walk in any direction results in fun — the Gaslamp Quarter to the north, the 446-slip San Diego Bay marina to the south, Seaport Village to the west, and PETCO Park to the east.

With 1,362 rooms in two 25-story towers, accommodations are as abundant as local activities. Pets of any size are permitted in any room for a $75 fee per stay. Guests' biggest predicament will be coaxing Fido from the plush guest bed when it's time to see the sights.

The Lobby Bar provides the perfect start to a relaxing vacation. Multiple flat-screens televise the latest sporting event. Tuck comfortably into a cushioned loveseat while sipping coffee or Cointreau. Inevitably, a few passersby will stop to pat your pup. Should guests want something more substantial than drinks, room service is the only option with Fido. The hotel's three eateries — DW's Restaurant, Roy's Hawaiian Fusion Cuisine, and LC's — do not permit

pets. No worries, a myriad of the Gaslamp Quarter's restaurants offer alfresco feasts. The hotel concierge will point hungry diners in the right direction.

THE WESTIN GASLAMP QUARTER

910 Broadway Circle, San Diego, CA 92101
(619) 239-2200 • www.westingaslampquarter.com ($$)
....

Adhering to the carpe diem attitude of pets, the Westin Gaslamp Quarter has few hard-and-fast rules for furry guests. Although there is a weight limit of 40 pounds, dogs exceeding this tend to get past the doorman. Once inside, the front desk staff present the pooch's owners with a welcome kit containing waste bags, plastic gloves, and a name tag on which to write their name and phone number.

None of the 450 guest rooms is off-limits to pets. A sink-to-the-snout Heavenly Dog Bed and food bowls assure canine comfort. A $150 refundable deposit and $35 cleaning fee are collected at check-in. Westin's two pet regulations require no canine be left alone in the room, and no pooches in the hotel's four eateries. A pet-sitter is the best option should parents decide to cool-out at the nightly "Unwind" party in the Lobby Lounge, or grab a meal at the hotel's Horton Bar & Grille.

The third-floor pool and deck redeems the hotel's few unkempt hallways and long elevator wait-time. Mutts and masters R&R on cushioned chaises and snuggle in downy towels. A verdant pocket park tucked among a jumble of downtown office buildings across the street is a good place to take Rover après swim.

A Westin WORKOUT six-page brochure is placed in each room with instructions on how to exercise your gray-matter with numeric brain teasers and word puzzles, as well as evening wind-downs of deep breaths.

HOTEL SOLAMAR

435 6th Avenue, San Diego, CA 92101 🐕 🐕 🐕 🐕

(877) 230-0300 • (619) 819-9500 • www.hotelsolamar.com ($$)

....

This boutique hotel is a member of the hip Kimpton brand, whose motto is "every hotel tells a story." The Solamar's story begins in San Diego's trendy East Village. Open just three years, it's already made a huge splash with the beautiful people.

The hotel's heartbeat is the lobby Living Room. Each morning and afternoon an eclectic group of guests convenes for complimentary coffee or wine, depending on the time of day. Cushy sofas play host to the impending relaxation. Conversation flows as freely as the libations. A number of partakers are escorted by furry friends. Canines curl up beside pillow-filled seating nooks, while owners take in the eye candy. Staff members gleefully sneak treats to visiting pooches.

Trend-setting decor doesn't stop in the reception area; it continues to the rooms. Sea blue walls, deep chocolate furnishings, and nautical accessories fill the space, with recycling bins giving a nod to the Green Movement. Leopard and zebra print robes reveal the hotel's racy side. All of the 235 rooms, except the tenth floor, are Fido-friendly, without a pet fee or size restriction. Dog beds and food bowls are delivered upon request. A "Do Not Disturb" sign, or "Shhh…I'm Working On My Inner Self" in the Hotel Solamar's case, is provided along with the pet "Paw"-licy outlining the hotel's dos and don'ts.

Judging from the size of the minuscule fitness room, exercise is not a priority. Or perhaps guests use the provided jogging map so they can see and be seen. The youthful clientele can replace a few workouts with in-room spa services, without repercussions.

Unfortunately, the hotel's excellent JSix Restaurant and J6 Bar can't accommodate pups, but pet-sitting is an option. It would be a shame to miss Chef Christian Graves's California cuisine, comprised of ingredients from nearby farms and fisheries, or the fourth floor, poolside outdoor J6 Bar, which has an anything-goes attitude; the perfect place to sip cocktails with locals.

SHERATON SUITES SAN DIEGO AT SYMPHONY HALL
701 A Street, San Diego, CA 92101 🐕🐕🐕🐕
(619) 696-9800 • www.sheraton.com/suitessandiego ($$)
....

Attached to San Diego's Copley Symphony Hall, this elegant high-rise is a classical music lover's dream. The all-suite hotel starts on the twelfth floor and reaches to the twenty-sixth, with floors one thru eleven designed for indoor parking. With over 100 concerts each season, the Sheraton hosts scores of symphonic enthusiasts.

Originally built in 1929 as a movie house, the Sheraton's Spanish-Colonial structure represents the more cultured side of San Diego. A formal décor of marble, mahogany wood, and high-back chairs fill the lobby. This doesn't deter traveling pets, who come along with

40% of guests in the summer months. Dogs up to 80 pounds can hone their sophisticated side free of charge. The 17th floor is reserved for furry friends, but this refined property will accommodate Fido on any floor, if asked.

As to be expected, rules are strict. No pets are allowed at the restaurants, the indoor pool and fitness center or alone in the room. There is no pup-sitting or walking available. Fido's consolation is a good snooze on the Sweet Sleeper Dog Bed. A gift shop off the lobby carries forgotten items such as dog food and chew bones.

Should two and four-legged guests want to head out to the nearby Gaslamp Quarter for dinner, a hotel town car is provided. Staying in? Schedule a spa treatment in the privacy of your room or order *en suite* dining and enjoy the slower-paced mode of travel.

TOWER23
723 Felspar Street, San Diego, CA 92109
(866) TOWER23 (869-3723) • www.t23hotel.com ($$)

....

South Beach meets San Diego at this avant-garde property. The Four Star hotel in Pacific Beach nuzzles the ocean, living the location, location, location axiom. Think minimalist when it comes to furnishing, described by the young, hip staff as "a clean contemporary celebration of the elements." Different colored neon lights play a large decorating role in the hotel, whose name is derived from a nearby lifeguard tower.

The Neo-Modernist theme is carried throughout the austere rooms. There is lots of chrome, glass, and wood. The pet-friendly rooms are on the second floor with access to the Tower Deck overlooking the beach. It is on this deck that pooch patrons take most their meals, as here and in-room are the two dining options for pups. The hotel's JRDN restaurant crew are happy to deliver breakfast, lunch, and dinner. Dog bowls and beds are not available, so  Fido will be sharing your Tempur-Pedic memory foam mattress. A one night fee of $75, or $150 for multiple evenings, is charged for pets no larger than 25 pounds.

Spa treatments at Tower23 are also in-room. Services and prices are on par with other high-end hotels. The Still Water massage is $120, a Koi Calm facial runs $145, and a Clear The Haze package (massage, facial and scrub) is priced at $335.

Tower23 has a unique offer; it is called the "Take Me, I'm Yours" package. A guest can "buy out" the entire hotel. It includes all 44 rooms, use of the Tower Deck, and whatever extras guests would like to add, such as cocktail parties or receptions. The cost is $13,955 for one night. A two-night minimum is required on weekends, somewhat steep for its younger clientele.

No animal I know of can consistently be more of
a friend and companion than a dog.

– Stanley Leinwoll

MARYJANE'S

207 5th Avenue, San Diego, CA 92101

(619) 764-6950 • www.hardrockhotelsd.com ($)

....

Hard Rock Hotel may not be pet friendly, but its retro coffee shop sure is. A saucy staff serves three squares, along with ooh's and ahhh's for the pooch. "Pot" brownies and cereal boxes at the table run a six spot, but a side of bad advice is free. Fans of compartmentalized dining frequent the Gaslamp hangout for MJ's TV dinner

of the day and counsel on a higher code to live by…never drink and blog…tequila makes you pretty…and always think twice before you pierce.

SAN DIEGO WINE & CULINARY CENTER

200 Harbor Drive; Suite 120, San Diego, CA 92101

(619) 231-6400 • www.sdwineculinary.com ($) • www.citydogsd.com

....

Gotta love a café that throws "Canines and Wine" gatherings every Wednesday from 5 p.m. to 9 p.m.. Locally produced, full-flavored varietals paired with Thai Flatbread Pizza or Spinach-Artichoke Dip make pooches and people drool. The expansive front patio overlooks Martin Luther King Promenade and San Diego's iconic Convention Center beyond. The City Dog Pet Shop raffles off treats and great prizes.

SAN DIEGO

BOMBAY EXOTIC CUISINE OF INDIA

3960 5th Avenue, San Diego, CA 92103

(619) 297-7777 • www.bombayrestaurant.com ($$)

....

An entryway waterfall cascading from the ceiling sets the Zen tone. Omnipresent brunette wood and demure lighting carry out the mood. Nighttime is especially beautiful. Curry infuses dozens of the Hillcrest locale's dishes. South Asian food is based on six tastes: salty, pungent, bitter, sour, astringent, and sweet. Bombay supplies them all. Diners who eschew meat appreciate the variety of vegetarian choices. It's customary to eat with your fingers, or with *Dahl* — Indian bread. The dog catches fumbled bites.

TERRA

3900 Vermont Street, San Diego, CA 92103

(619) 293-7088 • www.terrasd.com ($$)

....

The father/son operated bistro is tucked into the folds of Hillcrest, San Diego's bustling GLBT community. While most the neighborhood's restaurants line University Avenue, Terra's quieter location is

off the beaten path. It's expected that a AAA Three Star recipient prepares dishes of savory Cinnamon-Spiced Chicken and Butternut Gnocchi, but a pet menu as well? Yup, Terra's Tail Waggin' Specials satisfy even the pickiest of pooch palates. Peanut butter or beef "yapitizers," puppy pizza samplers, and doggie donuts keep Fido busy under the patio table for hours. Burp...

BURGER LOUNGE

1101 Wall Street, La Jolla, CA 92037

(858) 456-0196 • www.burgerlounge.com ($)

....

The ubiquitous gourmet burger chain keeps its menu short and simple with a Southern California flair. Four locations ensure the premium patties are merely a short drive away. Grilled turkey or vegetarian "quinoa" burgers rank as high as the Tallgrass beef. Chicken tenders, freedom fries, and two salads are the only additional items offered; cold brewskis wash it down. Makes it easy to decide what to share with the hungry hound.

KARL STRAUSS BREWERY RESTAURANT

1044 Wall Street, La Jolla, CA 92037

(858) 551-2739 • www.karlstrauss.com ($$)

....

The entire kit n' kaboodle started in 1989 when owners Chris Cramer and Matt Rattner solicited the tutelage of Cramer's brewmaster uncle, Karl Strauss, to introduce handcrafted beer to San Diego.

The rest is history. Countless suds and over 2,500 distribution points later, the "boys" have added "restaurateur" to their title. Signature ribs are napped with Red Trolley Ale BBQ sauce, and the salad vinaigrette boasts honey lager. The bacon on the club sandwich is brined in a secret amber marinade. All that's missing from the menu is "Bowser Barley" or "Mutt Malt" or "Snout Stout."

TRATTORIA ACQUA

1298 Prospect Street, La Jolla, CA 92037
(858) 454-0709 • www.trattoriaacqua.com ($$)

National accolades are showered on this Italian bistro in the heart of tony La Jolla — it's won USA Today's "Top 10 in America," Wine Spectator's "Award of Excellence" and "America's Top Tables" by Gourmet magazine. The chef serves no higher purpose than creating gifts from the sea, kneading homemade pasta, searing farm-fresh beef, and preparing locally grown produce. It's difficult to top his mussels cooked in white wine, herbs and crème fraiche. A foliage-filled courtyard with a trickling fountain and wicker tables bathed in white linen is the venue for diners with dogs.

PACIFICA DEL MAR

Del Mar Plaza
Pacifica Breeze Café, 1555 Camino Del Mar, Del Mar, CA 92014
(858) 509-9147 (Café) ($) • (858) 792-0476 ($$$$)
www.pacificadelmar.com

The bi-level restaurant stacks upscale Pacifica Del Mar on top of its casual Breeze Café. Both are delicious and have stellar views of the glistening sea. The second floor, Zagat-rated brasserie serves lunch and dinner. Their Dungeness Crabmeat Louis Salad is fresh and low-cal. A less healthy, yet equally tasty choice is the Zinfandel-Braised Short Ribs. Three alfresco tables accommodate dining dogs. Patrons of the downstairs, laid-back counterpart order breakfast and lunch at an inside counter, take a seat on the patio, and the waitstaff does the rest — which includes fetching water for mutts.

MILLE FLEURS
6009 Paseo Delicias, Rancho Santa Fe, CA 92067
(858) 756-3085 • www.millefleurs.com ($$$$)
....

Mille Fleurs has long been at the pinnacle of San Diego's fine restaurants. More than two decades ago, French-born Bertrand Hug culled his culinary talents and purchased a quaint restaurant in the exclusive Village of Rancho Santa Fe. Today, he has passed the torch to his son, Julien, whose goal remains the same — never have a customer want for a single

thing. It's this attention to detail, and Chef Woesle's determination to never wane in food quality and preparation, that continues to uphold the restaurant's reputation. Veal Kidney Sautéed in Green Peppercorn with Cognac and Smoked Salmon Belly with Potato-Cucumber Salad are examples of his talent. The atmosphere is casually elegant, and pooches are welcome on the courtyard patio.

Play

GASLAMP QUARTER WALKING TOUR
William Heath Davis House & Park
410 Island Avenue, San Diego, CA 92101
(619) 233-4692
www.gaslampquarter.org ($) • www.shopluckydog.com
....

Old West stories unfurl during this two-hour glimpse into the 16 square block Gaslamp district. Opium dens, gambling houses, naughty "ladies," Wyatt Earp, and more abound. The tour guide points out chi chi Z Gallery, which was once a pharmacy managed by Gregory Peck's father, who administered leeches for medicinal purposes. The area's longest-operating brothel has been converted into trendy Lucky Dog Boutique, selling canine accessories, art, and clothes. The defunct Chinatown now houses museums paying

homage to an instrumental cog of the city's history. Ardent dogophiles will love the two bronze statues of "Bum and Bobby" at the William Davis House. Bum, a Saint Bernard, was a steamship stowaway. He docked in the fledgling city in 1886, and was adopted by the townspeople. He officiated at parades and greeted dignitaries. Restaurants wooed customers with signs announcing, "Bum Eats Here." His counterpart was a Skye Terrier that belonged to a policeman in Edinburgh Scotland, a sister city of San Diego. Upon his master's death, Bobby sat by his grave for the remainder of his life, being cared for by nearby residents.

EMBARCADERO URBAN TREES

1040 1/3 West Broadway Street at Harbor Drive, San Diego, CA 92101
(619) 236-1212 (Visitor Information Center - Map)
www.portofsandiego.org/public-art
www.wheelfunrentals.com ($$)
www.gofishanthonys.com ($)
....

The Urban Trees outdoor art exhibit along San Diego Bay's esplanade is an ideal reason to leash up the hound for a stroll. Thirty abstract sculptures constructed from steel, blown glass, or wood, and spanning over 10 feet tall, are spaced along the two-mile path. The piece titled "Rolling Wilbur" features chrome balls dinging bells along a chain conveyer-belt, and the whimsical "SIC'Emore" has twirling copper canines. A poignant "Thank You" American eagle figurine, produced from U.S. military dog tags, rests in the sightline of aircraft carriers moored in the harbor. New "plantings" are rotated every year, availing previous pieces for purchase, most exceeding sums of $10,000. For those who feel the walk is lengthy, surrey four-wheel bike rentals help. Stop and dine among the statuettes at Anthony's Fishette's pet-friendly waterfront tables.

PETCO BASEBALL PARK

100 Park Boulevard, San Diego, CA 92101

(619) 795-5000 • http://sandiego.padres.mlb.com ($)

....

The San Diego Padres and PETCO retailers have joined hands, resulting in the most pet-centric baseball park in the nation. A mélange of pups and people converge on the East Village sport venue and its grassy environs on Game Day. Just beyond the outfield is the 2.7 acre Park At The Park, where pet posses gather to watch

America's favorite pastime televised on a huge screen just feet from the action. Gates open two hours prior to the game, inviting enthusiasts to peek at players during batting practice, and enjoy a box lunch at Picnic Hill. On promotional dates such as Dog Day of Summer, pooches are permitted into the stadium with the purchase of a ticket for the furry fan. Pet Adoption Day, held on Sunday home games, has found forever families for hundreds of pets.

CINDERELLA CARRIAGE RIDES

1604 Newton Avenue, San Diego, CA 92101

(619) 239-8080 • www.cinderella-carriage.com ($$$$)

www.seaportvillage.com • www.edgewatergrill.com ($$$)

....

Girls aren't the only ones who want to feel like a princess; pups do, too. Which is why Cinderella Carriage heeds their clarion call with pet-friendly rides throughout the Gaslamp Quarter and Embarcadero. Hulking draft horses named Suzy and Prince Charming clippity-clop a six-passenger, white filigree "pumpkin" along city streets for 30, 45, or 60 minutes, at the direction of a trained driver. A less ostentatious wagon minus the fairy tale ornamentation is also an option. Daytime jaunts pass San Diego's regatta of massive mili-

tary, cruise and historic ships; evening trips bare downtown's bustling nightlife. Tours start and end at Seaport Village, a 14-acre waterfront complex claiming more than 50 shops and a dozen restaurants. Pet-friendly Edgewater Grill's patio views of Coronado Bridge are enchanting.

WATER TAXI

1050 North Harbor Drive, San Diego, CA 92101

(619) 235-TAXI (8294) • (800) 44-CRUISE

www.sdhe.com ($)

....

Dog teleology purports that canines are jubilant when the wind is blowing in their muzzle, ears flopping in the breeze. If so, the water taxi on San Diego Bay is nirvana. A 31-foot retired Navy vessel ferries passengers to harbor hotels, restaurants, shopping, and Coronado Island; it's gratis for pups. The ride gives a beautiful vantage point of the city and the breathtaking skyline at night. On-call service runs Sunday through Thursday 9:30 a.m. to 8:30 p.m. Saturday and Sunday till 10 p.m..

SAN DIEGO'S 59 MILE SCENIC DRIVE
1040 1/3 West Broadway at Harbor Drive, San Diego, CA 92101
(619) 236-1212 (Visitor Information Center - Map)
www.sandiego.org • www.nps.gov/cabr ($)
....

Acclimate to San Diego with a 59-mile drive throughout its boroughs. Sightseers usually complete the leisurely route within three hours, with a few stops. The Visitor Information Center sells step-by-step directions with descriptions of the county's outstanding attractions. Cabrillo National Monument with its stellar views allows leashed pups at the Tide Pools. Nearby Haight-Asbury-ish Ocean Beach is a throwback to the 60s, with the antithetical upscale

Soledad Mountain a few miles north. La Jolla's UCSD campus represents a different architectural style with each building. The Geisel Library's inverted pyramid structure has a bronze statue of the Cat In The Hat creator, Ted Geisel, at the entrance.

WHERE YOU WANT TO BE TOURS
255 G Street #716, San Diego, CA 92101
(619) 917-6037 • www.wheretours.com ($$)
....

Husband and wife team Darlynne and Marc Menkin put the "F" in fun as they launch explorations throughout beach towns, city streets, and surrounding ravines. The Neighborhoods of Balboa Park Tour takes joy-seekers and happy hounds to historic Uptown, with its stately architecture and footbridges overlooking foliage-filled canyons. Bottled water and snacks are provided for the two-hour, pleasingly paced jaunt. If art and the jagged coast are more desirable, a "mutt-see" is the La Jolla galleries and seaside paths on the micro-region's walking tour. The twice-yearly "What Up, Dog!"

scavenger hunt encourages pups' inner Dr. Watson alongside their beloved owners' Sherlock, as they unravel clues around the Gaslamp Quarter.

BALBOA PARK
1549 El Prado, San Diego, CA 92101
(619) 239-0512 (Visitors Center)
www.balboapark.org

Balboa Park covers 1,200 acres in the center of San Diego. More than 130 years old, this playground's name honors explorer Vasco Nunez de Balboa — the first European to see the Pacific. It has hosted two World Expositions and housed Naval officers during WWII. Today, the pooch paradise is home to the world-famous San Diego Zoo, theaters, museums, and elaborate Spanish-Renaissance architecture. Nate's Point, Morley Field, and Grape Street off-leash "parkettes" offer Fido a little cardio. Cosmo's Doggie Blog on Balboa's website recommends permissible canine activities. His top

suggestions? The Botanical Building, Spanish Village artist colony, horticultural walking tours, concerts at Spreckels Organ Pavilion, picnicking at the Bea Evenson Fountain, and tea on the Japanese Friendship Garden patio.

LITTLE ITALY

India Street, between Ash Street and Laurel Street
San Diego, CA 92101
(619) 233-3898 (Little Italy Association) • www.littleitalysd.com
(760) 736-1138 (Little Italy Walking Tours) • www.littleitalytours.com ($)
(800) 91-GoCar • www.gocartours.com ($$$)
www.extraordinarydesserts.com ($$)
www.cohnrestaurants.com ($$)
www.busalacchis.com ($$-$$$)
www.carolgardyne.com
....

This Italian-American precinct epitomizes assimilation of one cul-
ture with another. Its linchpin is the Little Italy Association, which
assures cohesiveness of shop and restaurant owners and results in
one big happy family. The Busalacchi's are the big gumbas with four
lively eateries — Po Pazzo, Zia's Bistro, Trattoria Fantastica, and Café
Zucchero — all pet-friendly. Indigo Grill, Buon Appetito, and delec-
table Extraordinary
Desserts amore
poochies, too. Col-
orful history of
the urban quarter
unfolds on Antho-
ny Davi's Satur-
day "Behind The
Scenes" walking
tours. The tuna in-
dustry and Mafia
both had strong ties
to this 52-square-
block nascent hub.

Thrill-seekers can rent a bright yellow, three-wheeled, GPS-navigat-
ed GoCar with room for two, plus a small canine co-pilot, to tour
around the metropolis and beyond. Buono shopping abounds with
Juniper's mishmash of glam and clever home accessories. Hand-
painted silk fashions are Carol Gardyne Boutique's specialty. Trea-
sures of the Orient fill China's Seas.

OLD TOWN SAN DIEGO STATE HISTORIC PARK

4002 Wallace Street, San Diego, CA 92110

(619) 220-5422 (Visitors Center) • www.oldtownsandiegoguide.com

Old Town State Park contains a vivid history of California, from the Mexican occupation to the early American periods of 1821 to

1872, all huddled within a 15-acre compound. La Casa de Estudilla adobe hacienda displays lavish furniture purchased from ships passing through San Diego from Asia. There are lots of "firsts" in the park. Mason Street School was the first public schoolhouse in town, and the San Diego House saloon was operated by the first African-American settlers in San Diego. Park guides lead free, one-hour explorations to the past, recounting intriguing tales. Pups are restricted to the outside portion of the tours.

FAMILY KAYAK ADVENTURE CENTER

4217 Swift Avenue, San Diego, CA 92104

(619) 282-3520 • www.familykayak.com ($$$)

Pooches with a proclivity for open waters leap at the chance to hitch a boat ride with their paddling parents. Mission Bay, the largest manmade bay in the U.S.A., is just the conduit for hours of enjoyment in the cockpit of a recreational kayak. A one-mile private "Dog Paddle" takes pups and people past a blue heron breeding ground, where up to six nests are perched in each Torrey Pine. Next stop, Fiesta Island, where Rover runs with abandon along the sand. Guides lavish lots of TLC on the salty dogs. Max capacity per cruiser is two hounds and two humans, depending on whether the passenger is a Great Dane or Yorkie.

CORONADO

1100 Orange Avenue (Visitors Center)
End of Ocean Boulevard at North Island Navel Air Station (Dog Beach)
Coronado, CA 92118
(619) 437-8788 • www.coronadovisitorcenter.com
www.tentcityrestaurant.com ($$) • www.tartinecoronado.com ($$)
....

This quintessentially charming beach community definitely merits a visit. It was desolate until 1886, when investors saw the island's potential and built the famed Hotel Del Coronado, lovingly dubbed "The Del" by locals. The area blossomed in 1917 when sugar magnate John D. Spreckels sold a large plot to the U.S. government, and the Army, Navy and Marines moved in. In 1969, an expansive two-mile bridge was erected over the bay, making small-town America easily accessible from downtown San Diego. Forty years later, cottage-filled neighborhoods, world-class seashores, a clutch of mouth-watering cafes, and North Island Navel Air Station share 13.5 square miles. The immaculate, off-leash

dog beach continually ranks highest in the county. Waste bags and foot showers to rinse paws are provided. Diners laud the healthy cuisine at Tent City Restaurant, located in the Museum of History and Art building; pre-swim critters are welcome. Tartine's European café is another option, followed by a stroll down Orange Avenue to peek into the shops.

DEL MAR DOG BEACH

Highway 101, between 29th Street and Via De La Valle
Del Mar, CA 92014
www.delmar.ca.us ($ Pay-and-display)

....

Beside iconic Highway 101 is a sandy knoll known as "North Beach" to the locals of the affluent area. Pet owners are fastidious about maintaining the high integrity of this puppy playground. The crowd and their pups are courteous. Different times of year mandate different leash laws. October through May are off-lead. Summer months are more strict with the influx of tourists. Cleanup mitts are provided. Street parking with meters or an all-day pass from the pay-and-display ticket box is necessary.

TEMECULA VALLEY WINERIES

34567 Rancho California Road (Winegrowers Association)
Temecula, CA 92593
(800) 801-9463 • (800) 649-6463 (Sterling Rose Limousines)
www.temeculawines.org ($ tasting)
www.sterlingroselimo.com ($$$$)

....

No longer is it necessary to make the trek to Napa or Europe to experience impeccably produced varietals. Temecula Valley has

thrown its hat into the ring and is competing with the pros, with great success. The 25 wineries are as varied as their vintages — some casual and quaint, others expansive and elegant, many Fido-friendly. Sterling Rose Limos escorts pups and parents to taste the vintner's ambrosia. Oak Mountain Winery's Queensland Heeler, Pete, has his own label, "For Pete's Sake," with an image of the lovable lug donning sunglasses. His 2007 White is one of their best sellers. Mira, a black Newfoundland, surveys Miramonte's seven acres and escorts oenophiles to the tasting room for a sip of the Estate Syrah Gold Medal winner. Hart and Mount Palomar vineyards welcome amiable animals, but the alpha dog of friendliness is Baily's Winery, which hosts K9s on the restaurant terrace, and has a donation jug at the entrance for pet rescues.

SNUG PET RESORT

11339 Sorrento Valley Road, San Diego, CA 92121

(877) 345-SNUG (7684)

www.snugpetresort.com ($$ Daycare, $ Chauffeur)

....

Their slogan "feels like home, only better" is true, even if you're Snug owners LaDainian Tomlinson of the New York Jets and his

wife, Torsha. How many homes provide canine facials, massages, and aromatherapy treatments? The 22,000-square-foot facility raises the luxury quotient of doggie daycare. Dozens of employees monitor pups' whereabouts, whether they are swimming in the pool with friends their own size, rolling on the Easy-Turf lawn, or sniffing around the gift boutique. Chauffeur service to and from hotels is offered. Proof of vaccinations is required. A veterinary hospital is on property, assuring state-of-the-art care. So, go ahead, play a round of golf. Fido will be having a ball at the resort.

SPAWTIQUE MOBILE DOG GROOMING
(760) 815-0562

www.spawtiquegrooming.com ($$$$ varies with size)

Clients can relax poolside or at the hotel spa while pooches are being pampered in the Spawtique mobile pet salon. Groomer Suzy Korn is a licensed Registered Veterinary Technician and certified to clip the silkiest of tresses. All products are organic, non-toxic, and environmentally friendly, and a 50-gallon water tank guarantees warm H2O throughout the bath. Blow dryers coif unruly fur-dos – a godsend after a day at the beach.

Fetch

WESTFIELD HORTON PLAZA SHOPPING CENTER
324 Horton Plaza, San Diego, CA 92101

(619) 239-8180 • www.hortonplaza.com

An afternoon tryst at this outdoor mall is sure to leave guests with fewer presidents in their wallet. A labyrinth of 110 stores on four levels spans three city blocks in downtown San Diego. All genres are available, from upscale Louis Vuitton and Nordstrom to Banana Republic and teenybopper favorite, Forever 21. The top floor has Twenty-four restaurants, and fantastic views of the Gaslamp Quarter and Pacific Ocean beyond. Panda Inn has been serving delicious Chinese food for decades. The patio permits pooches.

UNLEASHED BY PETCO

308 Washington Street, San Diego, CA 92103
(619) 725-0850
304 East H Street #901, Chula Vista, CA 91910
(619) 691-0289 • www.unleashedbypetco.com

Unleashed is PETCO's cooler, more hip younger brother. They focus on premium, natural, organic and raw foods, along with other healthy pet lifestyle products. Knowledgeable employees dole out advice, holistic treats, and canine cuddles. Pugapalooza and Oodles

of Poodles parties, complete with doggie ice cream and photos, are just two of the festivities hosted for pups. In lieu of live pocket pets and a grooming facility, the neighborhood store has a cozy corner library with cushioned benches to sit and read fact-filled animal books, or fraternize with petable patrons.

CARLSBAD VILLAGE AND CARLSBAD PREMIUM OUTLETS

Intersection of State Street and Grand Avenue (village)
5620 Paseo Del Norte, Carlsbad, CA 92008 (outlets)
(800) 227-5722 (Visitors Center) • www.shopcarlsbadvillage.org
(760) 804-9000 • www.premiumoutlets.com
www.visitcarlsbad.com • www.bellefleur.com ($)
www.vigiluccis.com ($$$)

....

Carlsbad offers shopping in all shapes and sizes from quaint down-town boutiques to national retailers in an outdoor mall further inland. The Village is nestled between Buena Vista Lagoon and the Pacific. Bistros and art galleries share the sidewalk with antique stores and artisanal wine-tasting rooms. Scrumptious Italian cuisine is served on Vigilucci's Fido-friendly patio, overlooking the town's oceanfront promenade. Two miles southeast is Carlsbad outlet's trove of big brands — Gap, Banana Republic, Calvin Klein, et al, delivering hours of bargain hunting. Pups enjoy a languid break on Bellefleur's terrace while their parents survey purchases over lunch.

MUTTROPOLIS

Cedros Design District, 227 South Cedros, Solana Beach, CA 92075
(858) 755-DOGS (3647)
7755 Girard Avenue, La Jolla, CA 92037
(858) 459-WOOF (9663) • www.muttropolis.com

....

Co-founder Janet McCulley captures the Southern California mantra at this boutique by hosting occasional Doga Yoga classes for humans and their hounds. The Downward Dog pose is simple for most mutts. More difficult sun-salutations are demonstrated by Buddha, the yoga master's Bernese Mountain Dog. The annual February Smooch-A-Pooch fundraiser lets canine chums give big, wet licks at the kissing booth in exchange for a donation to the local animal shelter. Once a week, employees host breed-specific playdates. Four times a year, it's an "all-skate," with every variety invited to Yappy Hour.

Veterinarian

VCA EMERGENCY ANIMAL HOSPITAL AND REFERRAL CENTER
2317 Hotel Circle South, San Diego, CA 92108
(619) 299-2400 • www.vcaemergency.com
Open 24 hours, seven days a week.
....

VETERINARY SPECIALTY HOSPITAL
10435 Sorrento Valley Road, San Diego, CA 92121
(858) 875-7500 • www.vshsd.com
Open 24 hours a day, seven days a week.
....

The bond with a true dog is as lasting as
the ties of this earth will ever be.
– *Konrad Lorenz*

The natural beauty of the Southern California desert is breathtaking. Towering taupe mountains surge into a cobalt sky, and sandy basins sprout palm trees by the hundreds. Its vast open spaces are reminiscent of yesteryear, when life was unhurried and hanging out by the pool was considered a full day. The pace is slower here, more relaxed. Resorts accentuate this tempo and espouse leisure as the panacea for life's woes. They blend class and cool, resulting in a resurgence of tasteful Mid-Century décor throughout. Boutique properties have liberal pooch policies and larger hotels have walking paths to exercise canines. It's not uncommon to see a snout protruding from underneath many downtown bistro tables. The arid climate is tempered by sidewalk misters and ubiquitous air-conditioning. Winter months are more popular, as most summer days reach triple digits. No worries, that still gives you and your coddled critter eight months a year to visit this oasis.

PALM SPRINGS

Viceroy
Palm Springs

Riviera
Resort and Spa

San Giuliano
Hotel

San Bernardino

Parker
Palm Springs

Riverside

Corona

The Westin Mission
Hills Resort and Spa

Palm Springs

Indian Wells

Palm Desert

Lake Elsinore

La Quinta

Orange

Temecula

La Quinta
Resort and Club

Dana Point

Rancho Las Palmas
Resort and Spa

Hyatt Grand Champions
Resort, Villas and Spas

Carlsbad

Poway

VICEROY PALM SPRINGS

415 South Belardo Road, Palm Springs, CA 92262 🐕🐕🐕🐕

(800) 237-3687 • (760) 320-4117

www.viceroypalmsprings.com ($$$)

....

These people take pup lovin' seriously. For starters, the hotel logo is a sleek Whippet silhouette. The lobby is a wonderful jumble of upscale patrons sipping complimentary champagne, impeccably coiffed canines, and a manicured staff. Viceroy's black and white color palette, with bursts of lemon yellow, elevates the 1938 structure into the new millennium.

Poolside Citron restaurant is where two and four-legged guests loll happily in sunny paradise. Plastic dog bowls brimming with ice water are constantly refilled and can be personalized with your pooch's name as a keepsake. Pups even have their own menus consisting of a protein burger with veal stock, grilled chicken, and organic meatballs with pasta.

The Estrella Spa is beside one of the hotel's three pools. With the director's permission, well-behaved lapdogs can accompany bliss seekers into an outdoor treatment room and the relaxation lounge. Mani's and pedi's by the pool allow Fido and company to enjoy the property's Versailles-esque preened gardens.

The 67 rooms adhere to the troika color scheme with white as the dominant color. A few villas are monochromatic, showcasing white tile floors, walls, curtains, sofa, tables, armoires, towels, sheets, and so on, with a smidgen of black along the ceiling wallpaper. White dogs take heed for fear of getting lost in the décor. All pups, great and small, can stay in any casita for a one-time fee of $85.

LA QUINTA RESORT & CLUB
49-499 Eisenhower Drive, La Quinta, CA 92253
(760) 777-4800 • www.laquintaresort.com ($$$$)
....

The historic 45-acre labyrinth with 796 casitas is a town within it-self. A market, shops, restaurants, art gallery, hair salon, and spa all call La Quinta home, or more accurately, "country home," which is the translation of this desert landmark's name.

The original 1927 Spanish architecture was masterminded by Gordon Kaufman, who later went on to design the Los Angeles Times building and Santa Anita Racetrack. The lobby's exposed wooden beam ceiling and stucco walls look like Bonanza's Ponde-rosa Ranch kicked up a few notches. The entire resort manages to walk the fine line of understated elegance. It has hosted U.S. Presidents, countless Hollywood legends, and professional athletes over the years.

Mother Nature vacations here. It's evident with snapdragons

blooming among poppies and pansies, as black birds frolic in fountains and cicadas sing among the orange-blossom-fragranced air, all with the towering Santa Rosa Mountains as a backdrop. The Plaza is the best location to relax with the pooch, sip a cool beverage, and sink into the scenery. An extremely informative and fun one-hour walking tour of the property every Tuesday and Sunday morning meanders among this beauty, while a docent extols the resorts fascinating history. No reservations necessary, just meet in the lobby with your leashed pup.

Visiting canine chums are big, small, tall, short. There are no specifications except a $50 pet fee per stay. Dog beds and bowls are provided, along with a tote filled with goodies. Both the Adobe Grill and Twenty6 restaurant invite furry friends to dine with their families on the patio.

A well-heeled crowd in their middle-to-twilight years patronizes the resort, translating to empty-nesters who have reassigned nurturing to the family pooch. Pet-sitters are on call through Aunt Fran's Babysitting Service, freeing up guests to play a round of golf on one of La Quinta's five courses, take a dip in the resort's 41 pools, lob a few balls on the tennis court, de-stress with a Hawaiian Lomi Lomi massage, or dine sans doggie.

SAN GIULIANO HOTEL

375 West Arenas Road, Palm Springs, CA 92262
(877) 897-7100 • (760) 325-7100 • www.sangiulianohotel.com ($$)

....

"Comfortable" best describes this Spanish Hacienda. A friendly staff makes the eight-room boutique hotel feel like a private home. Originally purchased as a residence, the Italian owners decided to convert this unique estate into an oasis of tranquility.

A grassy courtyard with bougainvillea draped over room entry-ways, citrus trees dripping blossoms, and a towering 30-foot ficus tree is the hotel's hub. Here is where guests soak up the poolside sun, pets frolic, and new friends are made.

Each room has a different, yet similar style. Deep terra-cotta and cobalt hues stain the walls, although one suite is cream and white. Bathrooms maintain the Mid-Century burgundy and sherbet yellow tiles that are so Palm Springs. Outdoor living rooms, hot tubs, ornate fountains, or private lawns are a few of the amenities offered, depending on the room.

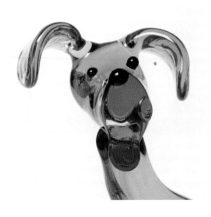

A pet welcome basket with Cesar Millan fortified H2O, Wild Cherry shampoo and spray, and a letter suggesting pet-friendly restaurants await Rover, along with Yin/Yang shaped food bowls and a cushy mat. The guidelines state "man's-best-friend" must be under 20 pounds, but a little birdie said larger dogs won't be turned away. A refundable $200 security deposit is required in case there is any damage. Otherwise, the rate is $30 a day.

There is no sustenance on the grounds, but kitchenettes in a few rooms allow vacationers to prepare their own meals. For those who've shunned the apron, a two-block walk to downtown offers a large selection of restaurants.

PARKER PALM SPRINGS
4200 East Palm Canyon Drive, Palm Springs, CA 92264
(760) 770-5000 • www.theparkerpalmsprings.com ($$$)
....

Gene Autry's Melody Ranch has been transformed into a hip hideaway. Thanks to New York designer Jonathan Adler's talent and meticulous attention to detail, The Parker is a work of art. The Palm Springs '60s signature motif is present with orange lacquered doors, zebra skin rugs, rattan hanging chairs, and huge, glossy red lips painted on the reception area wall. One look around verifies you're hanging with the "in crowd."

The lobby's indoor fire ring, encircled by Moroccan hassocks, way-lay plans to head directly to the guest room. Canine and company are invited to stay awhile and imbibe a fruity libation. Close by is Norma's restaurant, which offers alfresco lunch and breakfast. Dinner is left to Mister Parker's fine dining. No pooches permitted, but the concierge has a list of eager puppy-sitters.

Guests are eventually lured to the hotel's outdoor gardens, where lush Xeroscaping overflows onto pathways. Cushy chaises and bur-bling fountains fill secluded nooks and crannies. Eats and drinks are available anywhere on the grounds – in a hammock, under a palm tree, at the croquet lawn – anywhere. This ensures family dining with canine companions.

Fido's fee to enjoy this chic enclave is hefty – $150 a day. That's a lot of treats. The price includes a stuffed toy, bones, waste bags, and a pink bandana and bowls – for male or female sidekicks. No pup-pillows available; guest have to share their four-poster, glossy white beds.

Two saline pools offer a nice alternative to the usual chlorine-saturated hotel pools. For a workout, the hotel's spa - PSYC - offers a gym, treatments, yoga classes, as well as a casual attitude. Their manifesto claims you're only young once, but you can be immature forever. And post-workout cocktails are good for you. Obviously, The Parker Palm Springs has its priorities straight.

THE WESTIN MISSION HILLS RESORT & SPA
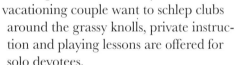
71333 Dinah Shore Drive, Rancho Mirage, CA 92270
(760) 328-5955 • www.westin.com/missionhills ($$)

One look at The Westin and it's easy to see why the desert is touted as "golf capital of the world." Not just one, but two superlative 18-hole courses offer hours of play on this 360-acre property. Choose from the Pete Dye or the Gary Player designed championship course. Both are award-winners from Golf Magazine and Golf Digest. Long fairways, elevated trees, and strategically placed bunkers challenge even the best golfers. Should only half of a

vacationing couple want to schlep clubs around the grassy knolls, private instruction and playing lessons are offered for solo devotees.

For those who like to relax, grab the pooch and a good book and head to Masters Plaza's sprawling terrace with cushioned chaises and views of the Dye course's eighteenth green. As loved ones play through, reclining cohorts can raise a glass of icy cold tea in solidarity. This location, along with the adjoining patio and fire-pit courtyard, is where mutts and their masters may eat, drink, and be merry. A popular place, considering almost 50 dogs a month stay at the resort.

Sixteen dual-level casitas house 512 guest rooms. One-and-a-half miles of paths meander along the park-like setting, providing ample walking opportunities. The pup's visit is "on the house," but they can't exceed 40 pounds. Bowls and a Heavenly Dog Bed will be waiting in the room upon arrival, as well as a Canine Concierge package from MANKINDdog with a blanket, leash, tennis ball, and treats. Guests must indicate a pet will be coming when booking reservations. Bellmen might be persuaded into taking Fido for early morning walks should pup parents not want to be seen pre-beauty regime. Pets are not permitted to be unattended in the room. A third-party sitter is available through the concierge, making it possible to spend a few hours by one of the three pools, play a game of tennis, or melt away stress at the spa.

HYATT GRAND CHAMPIONS RESORT, VILLAS AND SPA
44-600 Indian Wells Lane, Indian Wells, CA 92210 🐕🐕🐕🐕
(760) 341-1000 • www.hyattgrandchampions.com ($$$)
....

This AAA Four Diamond resort aimed for the top of the luxury market and hit the summit. Forty-three expansive acres have a litany of activities for multi-generations – a spa, fitness room, Camp Hyatt for kids 3-12, seven pools with cabanas, three tennis courts, and two golf courses, all with a jaw-dropping view of the Santa Rosa Mountains.

The 530 rooms range from deluxe to villas, the former being where most guests with pets stay because of the accompanying yard. Deluxe accommodations have patios and are located near the hotel's pet waste-station, providing bags for disposal. A one-time K9 fee of $50 is charged and a 35 pound weight limit is requested. Pet-sitting, dog beds, and food bowls are not provided.

Two hotel eateries welcome four-legged patrons on the patio – Lantana's California Cuisine and Pianissimo Lounge – each overlooking the tenth fairway. In true California style, Lantana will accommodate gluten-free, heart-healthy, and low-fat requests for breakfast, lunch, and dinner.

Pianissimo's alfresco lounge has live music at 9 p.m., Thursday thru Saturday. A Carmel Appletini or Cosmopolitan goes perfectly with silky jazz tunes. Bar munchies are served from 2 p.m. until midnight.

RIVIERA RESORT & SPA

1600 North Indian Canyon Drive, Palm Springs, CA 92262
(760) 327-3311 • www.psriviera.com ($$$)

....

The Riviera Resort & Spa has plucked hip from the early 1960s and sprinkled it on 24-acres in Palm Springs. A $70 million revamp of the Rat Pack's old hangout proves what's old is new again, only edgier.

Vibrant colors were the resort's muse, tangerine being the favorite. Keeping the desert's popular Mid-Century exterior architecture, the design team morphed only the property's interior decor. Ob-

scure lighting plays a huge role, with back-lit orange walls in the lobby and gargantuan pop-art chandeliers in Circa 59 restaurant. Floor-to-ceiling mirror tiles coax light to dance around the promenade off the entryway, as techno music reverberates throughout the space. Ebony vinyl chairs, fuscia velvet pillows, and crimson shag rugs complete the feel. The decorating *pièces-de-rèsistance* are eight Andy Warhol-ish art pieces made out of Guatemalan coins depicting the faces of Dean Martin, Frank Sinatra, and other legends.

Dogs 50 pounds or less are welcome at the coolest digs in the desert. The Riviera caters to the Los Angeles crowd and pooches are popular with the Hollywood set. A talcum-soft puppy bed, food bowls, and 100% Beef Hide Chews are provided in guest rooms.

Numerous garden areas surround the property, allowing furry friends to stretch their legs. One hundred dollars will cover Fido's visit.

The nucleus, heartbeat, core… whatever you want to call it…of the property is the pool. This is where everyone goes to "see and be seen," as well as catch a reprieve from the toasty Palm Springs heat. SoCalians are buff, so leave the flab at home. Tattoo-clad V- shaped men and artificially puffed women pose by the cement pond. In fact, the gift shop sells a cosmetic bag inscribed "I heart Botox." The poolside Bikini Bar offers over 50 rums and tequilas from around the world, assuring that anyone will look great after a few hours. Cabanas pay homage to former Miss America contestants with their kitschy photos hung among the chaises. Unfortunately, no dogs allowed – meaning the four-legged type – but pet sitting is available for $20 an hour.

Keeping with the laid-back mindset is SpaTerra, whose signature Balinese massage simultaneously applies Swedish, Chinese, and

Indian techniques with effervescent oils, culminating in utter and complete relaxation. In the age of ubiquitous pampering, it's refreshing to have a unique rubdown.

Without a doubt, no desert vacation is complete without a stay at this totally fun resort. One thing's for sure, you'll leave groovier than you arrived.

RANCHO LAS PALMAS RESORT & SPA
41000 Bob Hope Drive, Rancho Mirage, CA 92270 🐾🐾🐾🐾
(866) 423-1195 • (760) 568-2727 • www.rancholaspalmas.com ($$$)
....

This is family fun in a country club setting. Las Palmas has created a first-class atmosphere for all ages. Children can spend the day slip-sliding away at Splashtopia, a 1.2-acre water park situated in the heart of the 240-acre property, or at the adjacent Kidtopia camp. Adults can play a round of golf on the 27-hole course, or restore aching muscles at Spa Las Palmas. Pets are restricted from these activities, but the concierge will arrange a sitter.

The theme-park atmosphere of Splashtopia instantly draws youngsters to its 100-foot water slide and twisty 425-foot river ride where

guests lazily float on inner tubes throughout the playground. Tween music plays overhead as lifeguards slow the frenetic pace of little ones running among the water sprayers, pool, and sandy pseudo-beach. For a dose of serenity, seek refuge at the tranquility pool catering to those 18 and older, which is located at the opposite end of the resort.

The hotel's 466 rooms are in 32 separate buildings. Two buildings, totaling 20 rooms, are pet-friendly, only requiring a $100 fee and 45 pound weight limit. Pups get a 6" thick doggie bed and freshly baked peanut butter treats from the kitchen elves.

The sprawling grounds are ideal for brisk walks with canine chums. Depending on your pace, it can be a 2-4 minute hike to the lobby and its surrounding restaurants from the pet-friendly rooms. This totally embraces the "journey is the destination" thing, allowing guests to stop and smell the roses along the way.

Hounds and humans are welcome at the Palms Café, which serves coffee, salads, sandwiches, and other light fare on the patio from 6 a.m. until noon. Central Plaza, a charming terrace directly outside bluEmber restaurant, is the perfect spot for Fido and family to enjoy tapas and drinks at sunset while listening to live music.

Kibble

COPLEY'S ON PALM CANYON
621 North Palm Canyon Drive, Palm Springs, CA 92262
(760) 327-9555 • www.copleysrestaurant.com ($$$$)
....

Dogs dine among history at this classy 1947 bungalow once owned by Cary Grant. A huge willow tree weeps over a gurgling fountain on the terrace. White linen tables are interspersed among a cobblestone patio and  twinkling lights punctuate the evening sky where guests eat alfresco. The atmosphere is calm and relaxing. Purchased five years ago by the Copleys and Butterfields, the dinner-only bistro serves contemporary American cuisine seven evenings a week. Wait staff tout the "Oh My Lobster Pot Pie" as melt-in-your-mouth scrumptious; and the Parsley and Lavender Scented Roasted Rack of Lamb as over-the-moon. It's not hyperbole; the food truly is both.

SPENCER'S RESTAURANT

701 West Baristo Road, Palm Springs, CA 92262
(760) 327-3446 • www.spencersrestaurant.com ($$$$)
....

Four stars have been bestowed upon Spencer's Pacific Rim cuisine. Located at the base of the San Jacinto Mountains, the classy establishment's wealthy two and four-legged patrons arrive in Rolls Royces, Mercedes, and Range Rovers. A Zen feeling permeates the alfresco eating space with tables bathed in black linen, bamboo plants stretching skyward, a warming fire ring, and classical music trickling the air. Chef Eric Wadlund's illustrious career working

with such culinary icons as Eric Ripert of Le Bernardin in NYC prepared him to take the helm of the elite eatery. Visitors to Palm Springs will be hard-pressed to find such specialties as Beef and Veal Jumbo Tortellini, Pan-Seared Sonoma Foie Gras and American Paddlefish Caviar at any other restaurant. Bon appetite!

LE VALLAURIS

385 West Tahquitz Canyon Way, Palm Springs, CA 92262
(760) 325-5059 • www.levallauris.com ($$$$)
....

Zagat's food guide rates this French restaurant as "extraordinary to perfection; the gold standard in the desert with outstanding food, décor, and service." That's a lot to live up to, but Le Vallauris manages. The 1924 Roberson house is the perfect setting for this award-winning establishment. Do not miss the wine list, with over 250 selections, highlighting preeminent vintages worldwide – Haras Di Pirque from Chile, Australia's Shiraz Penfolds, and South Africa's Nitada Sauvignon Blanc, as well as French, American, and

Italian varietals. Savor King Salmon, Peking Duck, or Black Angus Ribeye Steak as moonlight filters through the patio's tree canopy. Petite pups who fit underneath the table are welcome to escort their owners.

PIERO'S ACQUA PAZZA
71-800 Highway 111
at The River
Rancho Mirage, CA 92270
(760) 862-9800
www.pierosacquapazza.com
($$$)
....

Piero's is waterside dining alongside a crystal blue, manmade lake at The River at Rancho Mirage shopping center. Leafy trees on the delightful terrace provide ample shade for pooches. The tables sport a ringside view of the nearby Santa Rosa Mountains. Embracing a "life is short, eat dessert first" attitude, the bistro bakes such decadent treats as French Crepes with Hazelnut Chocolate and Tiramisu, daily. The family-friendly atmosphere offers something for everyone, from white and red pizzas to Maine Sea Scallops and Plum Brandy Glazed Duck. Happy Hour is more like happy day, discounting drinks and apps from noon to night. Salud!

AUGUSTA RESTAURANT
73-951 El Paseo, Palm Desert, CA 92260
(760) 779-9200 • www.plazaroberge.com ($$$$)
....

Found in the posh El Paseo district, Augusta Restaurant is huddled in Denise Roberges's Plaza Roberge alongside her jewelry salon and art gallery. Pampered patrons dine among paintings and sculptures on the pet-friendly patio. The fare is as unique as the surroundings, with Squid-Dyed Black Ink Fettuccine and John Dory Fish in Crispy Philo. After your meal, stroll over to the jewelry workshop and watch goldsmiths create 22- karat pieces with precious stones and pearls. Pop in to the gallery where the architecture is art within itself.

OLD TOWN CELLAR

78015 Main Street, La Qunita, CA 92253

(760) 771-8950 • www.oldtowncellar.com ($$)

....

Placed in the heart of Old Town La Quinta, this restaurant's quaint patio boasts a handful of tables where patrons with pups can mingle over a glass of Donum Estate Pinot Noir or Napa Valley Barons IV Cabernet Sauvignon. Italian beer and Belgian Duval Ale please the non-wine drinkers. Tapas of Fig and Prosciutto Flatbread, or Gourmet Cheese and Imported Meats pair deliciously with the countless libations. A special-events calendar outlines wine-tasting schedules, live music agendas, and monthly discounts on varietals.

DESERT ADVENTURES ECO-TOURS
74-794 Lennon Place, Suite A, Palm Desert, CA 92260
(888) 440-5337 • www.red-jeep.com ($$$$)
....

Rusty, a 75 pound Nova Scotia Duck Tolling Retriever, and Lefty, a 65 pound Pit Bull, are the mascots for this fun tour company. Their proud parent and owner of Desert Adventures, Mary Dugan, describes them as "big, crazy, wonderful dogs." For 21 years, Dugan has steered adrenaline-junkies and their courageous canines in red Jeeps throughout a 1,000-acre private reserve in the Santa Rosa Mountains. Her Palm Springs Wind Farms tour investigates San Gorgonio Pass' massive windmills and their immense energy-producing turbine blades. Stargazers will be enthralled with the Night-watch Adventure, where guides use laser lights to identify con-

stellations, planets, and other luminaries. Out of courtesy, escorts ask fellow explorers if Fido can join the group. Although "no" is rare, a Rent-A-Guide private tour is optional for people with pets.

PALM SPRINGS MODERN TOURS
(760) 318-6118 • No website ($$$$)
....

Palm Springs "architectophiles" have restored scores of Mid-Century homes to picture-book perfection. Craftsmanship such as Donald Wexler's "spider leg" beams, and Albert Frey's signature steel and glass designs dot residential enclaves. Pleasures never pall on the three-hour, chauffeured Modern House Tour, where enthu-

siasts can peek at the exteriors of retro abodes. Indoor/outdoor living spaces, soaring rooflines, and carports are all iconic post-World War II traits. According to the National Trust for Historic Preservation, Palm Springs is one of the U.S.A.'s top 12 destinations to see such jewels. Guide Robert Imber's sure grasp of urban cool and sassy good humor leaves groups wanting more. Pooches can participate in two ways: ride along with fellow guests, providing all agree, or take a private tour for an extra fee. Either way, this is a must see!

PALM SPRINGS VILLAGEFEST
North and South Palm Canyon Drive,
between Baristo and Amado Road
(760) 320-3781 • www.villagefest.org

Every Thursday evening, nearly three blocks of Palm Spring's main drag transforms into a pedestrian esplanade with over 160 vendors. These are not the usual homogeneous street fair booths, but more trendy stalls with Guatemalan food, computer tech support, a rock climbing wall, golf course photography, even Republican and Democrat voter registration. Street entertainers and horse-drawn carriages jockey among henna artists, and handcrafted rag dolls. The VillageFest website promotes "We're Dog Friendly" in bold letters. Pups can pick up a custom-made outfit at Scooter Wear or visit Salt Water Licks for a puppy pastry.

TRINA TURK RESIDENTIAL
895 North Palm Canyon Drive, Palm Springs, CA 92262
TRINA TURK BOUTIQUE
891 North Palm Canyon Drive, Palm Springs, CA 92262
(760) 416-2856 • www.trinaturk.com
....

Trina Turk's adjoining housewares and clothing shops epitomize
upscale 1960s desert style. Retro wicker chairs and shag carpet
decorate both spaces. Colorful, abstract patterned clothing fills the
boutique, and needlepoint pillows, glassware, and kitschy knick-
knacks are sold at its sister store. Exceptionally groomed salespeo-
ple are helpful, but won't hover over shoppers and their soft-coated
sidekicks. The artfully crafted items don't need a salespitch. Unfortunately, the hip company hasn't tapped into the mutt market...yet.

THE CORRIDOR
515 North Palm Canyon Drive, Palm Springs, CA 92262
www.palmspringscorridor.com • www.kofficoffee.com
www.pawzps.com • www.digspalmsprings.com
www.bjustfabulous.com
....

One-of-a kind shops surround
a grassy courtyard where dog
owners and their precious
pooches come to play. Koffi
is the local gathering place,
serving all forms of coffee from
drip to Milano-style European.
Devotees sip joe, play board
games, and tinker on their
laptops. Catty-corner from
the java hangout is Paws pet
boutique, which donates 20%
of all profits to local animal
shelters. Next door is Digs,
specializing in unconventional
garden furniture and appur-

tenances. Quirky cards, books, and gifts are sold at Just Fabulous across the quad.

COLD NOSE, WARM HEART
189 South Palm Canyon Drive , Palm Springs, CA 92262
(877) 327-7747 • (760) 327-7747 • www.coldnosewarmheart.com
....
Cute name, cute store. Open for 11 years, these pup-pleasers traverse the spectrum with new gizmos and old favorites. The latest rage is faux ocelot pet pouches. It looks like a deep sack where small dogs can burrow for extra solace. Big dogs love TurnUp, an

odd shaped, hollow rubber ball, which bounces up, down, and all around. Beefy bones and cheesy scones are favorites of all critters. Colorful, limited-edition pooch prints and painted tiles line the walls. The Palm Springs spot is in the heart of downtown, making it a perfect walking destination.

EL PASEO DRIVE & THE GARDENS ON EL PASEO
Highway 111 and El Paseo, Palm Desert, CA 92270
(760) 862-1990 • www.palmsprings.com/elpaseo
www.thegardensonelpaseo.com

....

Think of this as "Rodeo Drive of the Desert." Escada, Bottega Veneta, and other fashionable boutiques line the 1.5-mile avenue, bestowing its reputa-

tion of the ultimate shopping destination. While the majority of stores greet pooches with smiles, Brighton Collections takes it one step further by placing a water bowl and treat jar at their entryway.

Tucked into a pocket of this exclusive district is The Gardens On El Paseo shopping cove. It is lushly landscaped with verdant plants, and the grassy lawns are peppered with playful bronze sculptures. Retail is less elite here, offering widespread chains such as J. Crew and Ann Taylor. Should you get carried away, a courtesy cart shuttles people, pups, and packages to their cars.

Veterinarian

VALLEY ANIMAL MEDICAL CENTER
46-920 Jefferson Street, Indio, CA 92201
(760) 342-4711
Open 24 hours, seven days a week

....

This Southern California borough's made-for-TV lifestyle has spawned the popular series *"The Real Housewives of Orange County."* Its 42-mile coastline stretches from Dana Point to Huntington Beach, with lots of luxury resorts, high-end shopping venues and gated communities in between. The residents are a mix of surfer dudes and ladies-who-lunch. But one thing is universal – they all love dogs. Whether they hang-ten at Huntington Beach Dog Beach with the pooch in tow, or get pup and parent massages at Casa Laguna Inn, it's a dog's life either way. In the land where an average house costs half a million dollars, there is no such thing as over-the-top. Carpe diem!

ORANGE COUNTY
DANA POINT • LAGUNA BEACH

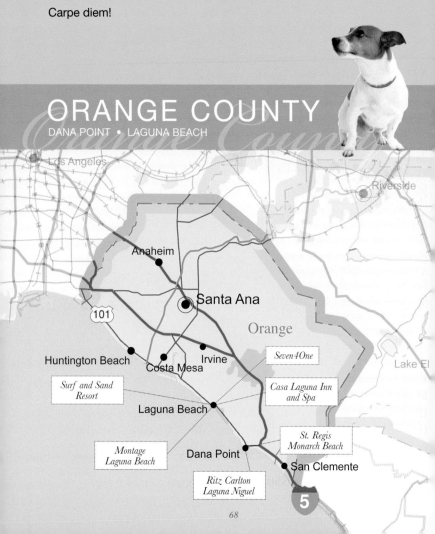

Los Angeles

Riverside

Anaheim

Santa Ana

101

Orange

Huntington Beach

Irvine

Costa Mesa

Seven4One

Surf and Sand Resort

Casa Laguna Inn and Spa

Lake El

Laguna Beach

Montage Laguna Beach

Dana Point

St. Regis Monarch Beach

San Clemente

Ritz Carlton Laguna Niguel

5

RITZ-CARLTON LAGUNA NIGUEL
One Ritz-Carlton Drive, Dana Point, CA 92629
(949) 240-2000 • www.ritzcarlton.com ($$$$)
....

Perched atop a 150-foot bluff, the Ritz-Carlton Laguna Niguel
boasts Pacific Ocean views nothing short of magnificent. Celebrating its 25th year of customer cosseting, the iconic resort is sporting
a new look with a total remodel. Traditional East Coast formal
décor has been replaced with sea blue walls and miles of gray-hued
marble.

A century has passed since Cesar Ritz masterminded the impeccable service the hotel chain adheres to today. The first Ritz-Carlton,
located in Boston, opened in 1927 with a room rate of $15. Thru
the years the Ritz has hosted countless two and four-legged celebrities, including Rin Tin Tin and Morris the Cat. Pampered paws
continue to prance throughout the properties.

A $150 cleaning fee and $50 per night lodging charge is the

poochie's initiation into the 418-acre Five Diamond playground. First floor rooms with access to expansive lawns and beach paths are Fido's "doghouse-away-from-doghouse," as the pet welcome letter states. The necessary bed, bowls, and bones are included. An in-room pet menu offers ground sirloin "Dog Bone Meatloaf" and chicken breast "Puppy Love." A better option is the small tables outside ENO restaurant, where waitstaff serve dining dogs.

ENO – short for oenology, meaning the study of wine – is an intimate wine, cheese and chocolate-tasting experience. Versed sommeliers passionately describe Old World earthy European wines and fruity American New World wines. They educate diners on whether the gold award-winner for best cheddar in the world, Fisciline, or the French edam-like Mimolette, is a better accompaniment. Dark chocolate ganache coated in coco powder and petite espresso sweets top off the evening.

Another Ritz decadence is the Buddhist Four Foot Ashiatsu massage. It costs $400, but break open the piggy bank if need be because this *acupressure-au-pied* is worth the price. Recipients are bathed in avocado oil, after which two practitioners simultaneously knead away aches and pains with the balls of their feet while suspended from wooden bars above the guest. Fellow masseuses Heather Christian, who jettisoned her aerospace engineering career for the massage table, and Michael Hempen invented this unusual technique. The procedure doesn't appeal to pups, but they're invited to accompany owners in an outdoor massage cabana, or the concierge can arrange a sitter for your little chum.

ST. REGIS MONARCH BEACH

1 Monarch Beach Resort, Dana Point, CA 92629

(949) 234-3200 • www.stregismb.com ($$$)

....

The crown jewel in Dana Point's tiara of hotels, the St. Regis is the only Five Star and Five Diamond property in the Golden State. Emblematic of cultured elegance, the 172-acre resort is both discreet luxury and California progressiveness. The 18-hole golf course, eight tennis courts, three swimming pools, kids' club, nature trails, 6.1-acre private beach, room butlers, surfing butlers, award-winning spa, and restaurants satiate guests' "I want it all" desires.

Pooches 30 pounds or less are greeted with a welcome letter extending the staff's wishes to "bow-wow" to the pup's every need. Furthermore, a pristine white dog bed with the St. Regis logo, dog bowls, and other necessities wait in the room; there's

even the latest issue of Doggie Aficionado magazine. The pet fee of $150 a day is hefty considering *le chien's* limited access to outdoor patios and other environs. The swimming pool bar, although not always open, and the Crust café, which sells coffee and light fare, are the two pet-friendly bistros. Room service is available or the concierge will arrange a sitter, should visitors want to dine at the hotel's six remaining eateries.

The guest suites are decorated in creams and browns. What they lack in character they redeem with a private terrace, walk-in closets and a huge bathroom. Door bells take the place of a simple knock, and nightly chocolates are delivered by extremely hospitable personnel.

Do take time to stroll the grounds. Magnificent stone fountains rivaling Italy's Trevily soar among date palms, spiraling junipers and pillared gazebos. Sweeping views span as far as Catalina Island many miles out in the Pacific.

CASA LAGUNA INN & SPA

2510 South Coast Highway, Laguna Beach, CA 92651 🐕🐕🐕🐕

(949) 494-2996 • www.casalaguna.com ($$)

....

This boutique inn is more understated than its hotel counterparts and is overflowing with loads of character. The initial dwelling was built in the 1920s as a caretaker's house to the adjacent Villa Rockledge Estate. Subsequent decades saw the addition of six bungalows, totaling 22 rooms, erected among tropical landscaping on a terraced hillside overlooking the Pacific Ocean.

The owners are enamored with canines, and have raised a few for Guide Dogs of America. This love translates into *mi casa es su casa*

for *perros*, allowing access to most of the property. Pets are welcome at breakfast and afternoon wine hour, both served in the original Mission House. New acquaintances are forged with fellow guests while dining around the living room fireplace. Alfresco alternatives are the Palm Court, huddled among lush foliage, or the Sunset Patio with its stellar ocean views.

Pampering headquarters is on the Garden Terrace. Here humans and hounds can partake in a "Togetherness Massage" for either two people and a dog, or one guest and one pooch. An appointment is necessary; the inn uses a third-party licensed canine masseuse. Terry Senko, President of Pawsitive Feelings, kneads the pup's back legs and shoulders, manipulates ears with delicate strokes, and checks paws for proper circulation. Large breeds take 45 minutes, smaller ones 25 minutes. On chilly days the service is performed in-room or in the spa. There is an extra charge from the nightly $25 pet fee, but it's well worth it.

SEVEN4ONE

741 South Coast Highway, Laguna Beach, CA 92651

(949) 494-6200 • www.seven4one.com ($$)

....

This ultra-contemporary 12 room hotel has pulled sleepy Laguna Beach into the 21st century. No signs of the property's prior life as a B&B and flop-house remain. The two owners have fashioned it after a European hotel, focusing on customer service and engaging every visitor. Before arrival, guests fill out a profile via e-mail stating pillow choices, coffee/tea preferences, and in-room needs such as a flat-iron, make-up mirror, and the like.

Seven4One is the first certifiably green hotel in Orange County, reducing its carbon footprint in building elements and operations. Keyless PIN activated door locks eliminate plastic cards, large windows utilize SoCal's natural light, and washable glasses as well as no plastic water bottles are just a fraction of the steps taken. Couple this with the restaurant's organic tapas and natural adult spirits, and you have a Green Hotel Association of America member.

Seven4One doesn't have a traditional reception desk check-in. Instead, a Guest Experience Manager, or GEM, meets travelers in the foyer and escorts them to their rooms giving a short tour along the way. These personal butlers buzz around the hotel catering to guest's whims, whether it be, arranging spa treatments, or setting up towels, chairs, and umbrellas at the nearby beach, returning every 30 minutes with cold water and a reminder to turn over.

It's apropos that this small hotel only allows small dogs. A nominal $35 pet fee per stay allows lap-pooches to be lavished with walks, toys, and even a custom made bed of down-feather pillows and eco-friendly, super soft cotton/bamboo sheets. No area is "off-limits"; pups can join parents in the lobby for cocktails and snacks, or perhaps a siesta on the second floor sun deck. The intimate, first floor courtyard is equally inviting; by day the space pipes out re-corded music, by night silent movies are projected on the east wall.

MONTAGE LAGUNA BEACH
30801 South Coast Highway, Laguna Beach, CA 92651
(949) 715-6000 • www.montagelagunabeach.com ($$$$)
....

There is no need to extol the resort's grand lobby, 250 oversized guest quarters, marble bathrooms, estate-quality furniture, award-

winning dinning options, and impeccable attention to aesthetic detail; this is expected in a Five Star hotel. What does bump this Craftsman-Style beauty into another echelon is the kindness of their exemplary staff. Most high-end resorts brag about customer service; Montage leads by example.

When pups and their parents check in, a fresh-faced receptionist gleefully pulls out a Radio Flyer wagon full of dog toys from behind the desk. Fido chooses a favorite while rubs and tickles are bestowed upon the fuzzy guest. Treasure in tow, travelers are ushered to a first-floor room with a pranceable, verdant lawn. A trundle dog bed with a drawer to store bowls and treats sits by French doors leading to a spacious patio.

Personalized greetings throughout your stay from passing employees are plenty: "How is your stay, Ms. Espinosa?", "Is there anything I can assist you with, Ms. Espinosa?" No doubt one of the reasons Montage has collected more than 60 awards, including "Top 100 Hotels in the World" from Travel & Leisure magazine.

The Lobby Lounge, where pups are permitted at the peripheral tables, has live entertainment nightly. Waiters chitchat with guests, suggesting the best drink selection for individuals, whether it be an herbal elixir, cocktail, or H2O from their water menu. One of the 17 choices of agua from Europe, North America, and the South Pacific is sure to quench anyone's thirst…even the pooches'.

A lobster hoagie from the Mosaic Bar & Grille will soak up some of that liquid. The terrace does not allow pets, but the chef is happy to prepare a take-out meal . The 30-acre resort has numerous picnic spots. The large fire ring surrounded by Adirondack chairs on the bluff overlooking the Pacific Ocean offers perhaps the best view in the house. Should you want to dine at the signature restaurant, Studio, pet-sitting is available.

If you don't hire a sitter for a night out, do be sure to use the service for a day at the spa. Three words say it all…surrender, relax, rejuvenate.

SURF & SAND RESORT

1555 South Coast Highway, Laguna Beach, CA 92651
(949) 497-4477 • www.surfandsandresort.com ($$$)
....

If this hotel were any closer to the Pacific Ocean, guests would swim to their rooms. Located smack-dab on the beach, this Four Diamond resort is a real treat. A color palette of sand-hued marble and ecru-painted walls folds the 165-room seaside beauty into its shoreline environment.

Views from the room's private balcony span the horizon. Sailboats in the distance are mere dots in the azure sea, and the sensory experience of crashing waves, singing seagulls, and fragrant briny air

is everywhere. Nearby cliffs display million-dollar homes of locals who have achieved the American dream; yet a stay here is a close second.

Dogs 25 pounds or less are welcome. In exchange for $100 per stay, they can romp on the beach, lunch on the Ocean Terrace, and hang at the Pacific Perk coffee shop. No beds or bowls are available, but the helpful housekeeping staff will supply disposable ice-buckets cut down to the proper eating height for your pup.

Pet-toting travelers need not forgo the resort's signature hot shell massage. An Aqua Terra Spa therapist will bring the polished South Pacific clam shells to the room and soothe tired muscles for 75 minutes. While you're at it, go all-out and soak the remainder of the day away with an aromatic bath ritual offering a choice of five different scents. After all, what's your hurry?

Kibble

SAPPHIRE LAGUNA RESTAURANT AND PANTRY
1200 South Coast Highway, Laguna Beach, CA 92651
(949) 715-9888 • www.sapphirelaguna.com ($$$)

Chef Azmin Ghahreman has obtained gastronomic excellence with his premier restaurant, Sapphire. The culinary maestro's past 20 years of cooking in Australia, Malaysia, Singapore, and Turkey have culminated in a global menu with dishes to please any palate. Tapa-style Spice Plates sing on your tongue with seasonings from around the world. Curried Barramundi is a favorite. The Salt and Pepper Hong Kong Shrimp with cilantro, jalapeño and chili has a kick. With a dozen choices, make sure to try more than one.

Bartenders churn out the signature Buddha's Hand Margarita with a dollop of lemon marmalade for extra zing. The restaurant's atmosphere is savvy chic, minus the pomp and pretentiousness of other establishments. The patio, which

affords an outlying sea view, usually has a furry snout protruding from underneath one of the tables. The adjacent Sapphire Pantry gourmet shop will assemble a picnic basket for a day at the beach with wine, cheese, cured meats, and prepared salads.

MADISON SQUARE & GARDEN CAFÉ

320 North Coast Highway, Laguna Beach, CA 92651
(949) 494-0137 • www.madisonsquare.com ($$)

....

Owner Jon Madison loves dogs, so eleven years ago he opened a home-store-cum- courtyard-café, where patrons could bring their precious pups. The seventh-generation New Yorker overhauled a 1912 Craftsman bungalow to perfection, and drew from his prior

career as a landscape architect to create a garden with almost 300 rose bushes, soaring hemlocks, and a Koi pond surrounded by succulents. His impeccable taste results in products both whimsical and exquisite, like Rubenseque garden statues perched beside playful dog ornaments and bird houses. Madison's affection for animals transcends canines. Photos of his three sponsored African baby elephants are displayed behind the shop's counter in the vein of children's school pictures. "Simon," as Madison lovingly calls the wild possum who hangs out on the property, is fed Meow Mix and avocados. Diners are treated equally as well with breakfast and lunch specials from 8 a.m. until 3 p.m., Monday through Saturday. Like Simon, you'll never want to leave.

FRENCH 75 BISTRO AND CHAMPAGNE BAR

1464 South Coast Highway , Laguna Beach, CA 92651
(949) 494-8444 • www.culinaryadventures.com ($$$)

....

The restaurant's name is taken from a drink conjured up during WWI. French soldiers swigged a potion of champagne and cognac from 75-millimeter cannon shells, and kaboom…it hit them like a mortar. Today, guests sip the sparkling elixir out of crystal flutes with a dash of sweet and sour mix. The dinner-only bistro has a Bubbly Hour six evenings a week, inviting guests to try their signature cocktails for half-off. The brick outdoor patio parlays the restaurant's "1940s Paris After Dark" theme with heavy wrought-iron tables draped in white linen, a fireplace, chandeliers, and jazz music playing overhead. *Chiens* can rest comfortably alongside diners as superb dishes of Duck Confit, Coq Au Vin, and Lobster-Fromage Blanc Ravioli are served…ooh la la.

SUNDRIED TOMATO CAFÉ
361 Forest Avenue, Laguna Beach, CA 92651
(949) 494-3312 • www.sundriedtomato.biz ($$$)
....

Sundried has been a mainstay in Laguna for over a decade. The bistro's courtyard splays onto trendy Forest Avenue, placing diners and pups in the middle of the social scene. Guest's slurp up delicious bowls of creamy Sundried Tomato Soup with Gorgonzola Cheese, while their sidekicks lap a bowl of cold water; a win-win situation. Burger devotees love the flavor-packed Lamb Cheese Burger, a new twist on an old favorite. The irrepressible pouring hand of the bartender yields chocolate martinis, or Pinocrano's – a drink of pineapple-infused blue iced vodka with a splash of cranberry juice. Tamer libations of

pinots and chardonnays, or Chimay draft are another option. Adoration runs deep for this place, spurring the owners to open two other locations south of Laguna, in San Juan Capistrano and San Clemente.

ZINC CAFÉ & MARKET

350 Ocean Avenue, Laguna Beach, CA 92651

(949) 494-2791 • www.zinccafe.com ($$)

....

This vegetarian restaurant shrouded behind a leafy hedge is well worth a visit. The food is so scrumptious there's no need for bells and whistles. It's where the wealthy, who can afford any meal, go to eat when they crave uncontrived, healthful dishes. At any given time there is at least one pup on the garden terrace eagerly eyeing delicacies of Potato Pancakes with Apple Sauce and Sour Cream, or Quiche and Lemon Vinaigrette Salad. Doors open at 7 a.m., inviting you to pry open morning peepers with a strong cup of joe and a Cucumber Salsa Breakfast Frittata. With the recent addition of dinner and live music Wednesday through Sunday, Zinc is now serving from sunup to sundown.

LAGUNA CULINARY ARTS

845 Laguna Canyon Road, Laguna Beach, CA 92651

(949) 494-4006 • www.lagunaculinaryarts.com ($$)

....

Tucked away in a strip mall a mile outside of town, this cooking school/gourmet wine and cheese shop is upscale without the glamour. The small café hosts a trip around the world for your taste buds. A 20-plus item menu is comprised of quality sandwiches and salads made with French cow's milk cheeses, sheep milk blends from Catolonia Spain, olive muffaletta, and spicy pork sausage. The server will suggest a food-friendly wine to accompany any selection and is happy to wait on patrons and pups lunching at

the outside tables. The shop sells more than 100 cheeses ranging from obscure lavender and coffee-coated to the familiar Gouda, the most expensive being Beill Tomme Brulee hovering around $40 a pound. Should you fall in love with one in particular, they will ship.

LOS RIOS HISTORIC DISTRICT

Los Rios Street, between Del Obispo and Mission Street
San Juan Capistrano, CA 92675
(949) 493-8444 (Historical Society)
www.sjchistoricalsociety.com • www.sanjuancapistrano.org

Located less than ten miles from Dana Point, Los Rios Street is the oldest preserved residential road in California. Thirty-one houses dating from the 1800's line a four-block lane canopied by mature trees. Three of the original adobe structures built in 1794 remain; additional homes are circa 1887 to 1910. The Rios Adobe is occu-

pied by the tenth-generation Rios family. Other dwellings contain small shops and cafes in the front portion, with the residents living in the back. The owner of The Ramos House Café lives and works on the property, grows his own herbs, and churns ice cream daily for the customers. The front porch tables host hounds, and the chef offers BBQ Chicken Salad with Hush Puppy Croutons. Walking maps are available at the nearby railway depot platform. Don't leave without exploring nearby downtown Capistrano.

DANA POINT HARBOR
34624 Golden Lantern Street, Dana Point, CA 92629
(949) 923-2255 • www.danapointharbor.com
....

Soak up the sun with a stroll along the Dana Point waterfront.
Over three miles of pathway hug the man-made harbor. Nautical
peeps and their pups can explore the East and West Basins on a
skiff or sailboat rented at the Embarcadero Marina. Three yacht

 clubs call the seaport home,
providing guest slips for
those who are visiting Dana
Point on their private crafts.
Holiday boat parades com-
plete with children's games,
music and Santa, as well as
the Tall Ships Festival with
tours of the historic vessels
and storytelling create family
camaraderie in the charming
shore town.

THE COTTAGES AND BUNGALOWS OF LAGUNA WALKING TOUR
Laguna Beach Visitors and Conference Bureau (Map)
252 Broadway and 381 Forest Avenue, Laguna Beach, CA 92651
(800) 877-1115 • www.lagunabeachinfo.com
....

The City of Laguna Beach Heritage Committee created a thor-
ough self-guided walking map, steering visitors on a journey of
the city's architectural past. Featured are fifteen privately owned
bungalows in the north portion of the city, ranging from 1907
to 1933, and fifteen cottages in the south side of Laguna dating
from 1884 to 1939. The bungalow tour covers eight blocks, and is
an easy walk with 0.40-miles being the longest distance between
homes. Southern cottages cover 13 blocks. The humble dwellings
epitomize Laguna in its infancy, featuring Craftsman, Colonial,
Tudor, and Chateau styles. Tidbits about Hollywood stars, artists
and high-powered businessmen who once lived in the dwellings accompany the map. Canine chums will love the stroll.

FIRST THURSDAYS ART WALK

Laguna Beach Visitors and Conference Bureau (Map)
252 Broadway and 381 Forest Avenue, Laguna Beach, CA 92651
(949) 683-6871 • www.firstthursdaysartwalk.com
....

The first Thursday of every month, from 6 p.m. until 9 p.m., Laguna's trove of art galleries pop the wine cork, start up the music, and throw open the doors for a free exhibition of their finest pieces. Abstracts, wall sculptures, photography, etchings, and other mixed media are showcased. Laguna's prized "Plein Air" Monet-style impressionist paintings of landscapes – which originated in the area – are demonstrated by local artists in numerous shops. The 40-plus participating galleries cover a two-mile span through-out the north, central, and south parts of town. Shouldn't wear out pups too much. The Visitors Bureau provides Art Walk brochures and maps.

MAIN BEACH

Pacific Coast Highway at Broadway and Ocean
Laguna Beach, CA 92651
....

As the name implies, Main Beach is THE beach in Laguna. Stretched alongside the Pacific Coast Highway in the heart of the village, Main's proximity to nearby shops and bistros makes it popular with tourists and locals. At any given time, a SoCal sand sport is being enjoyed here, whether it be volleyball or body surfing.

Fido's seaside hours are restricted, depending on the time of year. Winter months – mid September through early June – your furry friend can saunter in the sand all day long on a leash. Summer months – early June through mid September – your

leashed love can enjoy the salt air before 8 a.m. and after
6 p.m. A wooden boardwalk running the length of Main keeps
paws relatively sand free. The same rules apply to the 22 public
beaches running Laguna's seven-mile coastline, except for Aliso
Beach Park, where no dogs are permitted.

Fetch

LATITUDE 33 BOOKSHOP
311 Ocean Avenue, Laguna Beach, CA 92651
(949) 494-5403 • www.latitude33bookshop.com

This "fiercely independent" bookstore – as it refers to itself – is
a reader's dream. The name is derived from the shop's location
within the 33rd latitude. Open 12 years so far, fans will make sure
it survives and thrives despite the mega-bookstore phenomenon.
Budding authors and widely published manuscripts share shelf
space. Employees read new releases and place their hand-written
comments on an index card beside the book, giving a first-hand account of the volume's pace, depth of characters, and visceral quality. Latitude 33, as with other indie stores, lends itself to impromptu discussions with staff or fellow patrons. Pooches are welcome to

hang out as you discuss travel genre pieces such as Adam Gopnik's account of his time abroad in "Paris to the Moon" or J. Maarten Troost's hilarious book about his South Pacific two-year stint, as reported in "The Sex Lives of Cannibals."

UPSIDE DOWN

1432 South Coast Highway, Laguna Beach, CA 92615
(949) 376-2012 • www.upsidedownfashion.com
....

Strange name, cool shop. Ornate chairs and flowering trees hang upside down from the clothing store's ceiling, hence the moniker. Yugoslavian owner Zel Pehar and his Bosnian wife joined their collective fashion smarts, culminating in a showroom of hot European couture. Both are dog lovers and keep healthy treats behind the counter for Fido fashionistas. Dresses from French designer Cop Copine mingle perfectly with bohemian clothing from Spanish and German lines. Racks hold two or three of each style, so as not to saturate the market. A Manhattan Beach artist custom-makes tote bags for the boutique from discarded newspapers.

Their George, Gina & Lucy handbags accessorize stylishly with the Gee WaWa platform shoes, all at price points under $300.

MUSE

300 Forest Avenue, Laguna Beach, CA 92651
(949) 497-7026

....

They have no website and their online advertising is a MySpace page (Muse Boutique Laguna Beach), signifying the level of trendiness. The shop is roomy and not jammed with inventory; ideal for you and your K9 to browse. The celebrity fave Wild Fire raglan tees and Boy Meets Girl racer back tanks are hot sellers. Recycled cotton totes, leather flats, jeweled headbands, earthy body sprays, and funky belts represent the lifestyle Muse parleys. Prices range from "Wow, that's a deal" to " Let me think about it." The fun, girly staff assists, but doesn't linger. Fashions are updated every week, assuring the latest and greatest.

BARK AND SNIFF BOUTIQUE

1330 South Coast Highway, Laguna Beach, CA 92651
(949) 715-DOGS (3647) • www.barkandsniffboutique.com

....

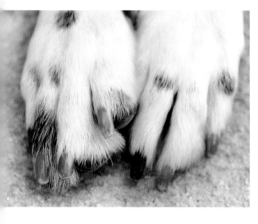

Here's shoppertainment for mutts and masters. Gina, the owner, believes all dogs should be pampered and she has an avalanche of accessories to make it happen. For starters, nail "pawlish" for pups. The polish manufacturer, OPI, has a line of colors catering to "nails for those with tails," as their slogan quips. Bow Wow Green, Dog House Blues, Poodle Pink, and Yuppy Puppy are a few shades. Once you've chosen the correct hue for Fiffi's complexion, pick up a soy aromatic candle to burn during the in-home mani-pedi. A Swarovski crystal collar will complete the look. Squeaky toys fashioned after top shoe designers "Dolce and Grrrrrbana," "Jimmy Chew," and "Bark Jacobs" are so in. Less glitzy hounds will enjoy the more classic argyle or paisley collection of neck apparel. There is something for everyone.

CROWN VALLEY ANIMAL CARE CENTER
28892 Crown Valley Parkway, Laguna Niguel, CA 92677
(949) 495-1123 • www.crownvalleyah.com
Open 7am to 11pm, seven days a week

We long for an affection altogether ignorant of our faults. Heaven
has accorded this to us in the uncritical canine attachment.

– George Eliot

Dogs laugh, but they laugh with their tails.

– Max Eastman

Anaheim

The Shorebreak
Hotel

101

Santa Ana

Wyndham
Orange County

Huntington Beach

Costa Mesa

Irvine

The Westin
South Coast Plaza

Lake Elsir

Hilton Waterfront
Beach Resort

Island Hotel
Newport Beach

Newport Beach

Balboa Inn and
The Resort

The Balboa Bay
Club and Resort

Fairmont
Newport Beach

Dana Point

San Clemente

Stay

THE BALBOA BAY CLUB & RESORT

1221 West Coast Highway, Newport Beach, CA 92663
(888) 445-7153 • www.balboabayclub.com ($$$)

Few hotels have a 125-foot Baglietto Italian yacht moored at the back door. Ballissima is her name, and she is owned by the ex-Prime Minister of the former Yugoslavia. This is only one of the nautical beauties who call the Balboa Bay Club & Resort home.

Established 60 years ago as a private boating club with notable celebs such as Humphrey Bogart, Bing Crosby and Bob Hope, the 15-acre property expanded in 2003 to include a 160 room resort perched alongside Newport Harbor. Photos of the Hollywood cronies line the hotel's "Wall of Fame" outside "Duke's Place" bar, named after past member John Wayne.

Maritime mutts, 25 pounds or less, are welcome for 25 clams a day. The resort's seamanship extends to pooches, offering electric Duffy boats for pups and their parents to rent. Concierge Patrick Hynes – who, by the way, is one of only 520 United States members of the prestigious Les Clefs D'Or concierge society – can arrange for a picnic to be delivered to the craft. With top speeds of seven miles per hour, almost anyone can captain

the 21-footer around the bay. Check out the million-dollar ships, such as the Don Juan, which is large enough to hold another vessel named Don Juanito.

After cruising the waterways, have a drink in the hotel's Library with your furry first-mate. Not a lot of books, but plenty of fireside superluxe sofas, and views of the marina. Unfortunately, neither of the two restaurants is accessible to pets, but Patrick can orchestrate an alfresco feast on the outdoor benches overlooking the harbor… SoCal style.

ISLAND HOTEL NEWPORT BEACH
690 Newport Center Drive, Newport Beach, CA 92660
(949) 759-0808 • www.islandhotel.com ($$)
....

This Five Diamond hotel is sophisticated and Southland casual. With 20 stories, pet people can choose a higher floor with killer views of Newport Harbor, or a lower room with easy access to the large green lawn beside the tennis courts.

The "Pampered Pet Package" provides homemade treats, a plush 30"-square dog bed exhibiting the Islands' Bird-of-Paradise logo, food bowls with painted palm trees, and bottled water. It even includes a fruit plate for the parents. The hotel's $100 pet fee is buried in the package rate. Weight limit is 50 pounds or less.

Island's Palm Terrace restaurant kicks the three squares up a notch with Chef Bracken's delicious twist on the usual. Banana-Stuffed Brioche French Toast or Mac and Cheese with washed-rind Italian Taleggio, crushed truffles, and parmesan tuile are sure to get the taste buds salivating. Pups can join guests on the Palm's tropical outdoor patio.

Libations flow from 5 p.m. to 7 p.m. during the lounge Social Hour. Small bites and drinks are priced according to the time...$5 at five o'clock, $6 at six o'clock and $7 at seven o'clock, so get there early. A pony wall delineates the lounge from lobby seating where guests with pets must sit – health code rules.

For those who want to stretch their gams, the concierge has a jogging map in the shape of a sneaker for easy portability, navigating 1.5, 3 and 6 mile routes through the Newport Bay Ecological Preserve. Or "hike" next door to the Fashion Island outdoor mall to walk off chef's Valrhona Manjari Chocolate Obsession.

BALBOA INN AND THE RESORT

105 Main Street, Balboa, CA 92661

(877) BALBOA9 (225-2629) • (949) 675-3412

www.balboainn.com ($$$)

....

Getting to Balboa Inn and The Resort is half the fun of staying there. Located on the western-most promontory in Newport Beach, a three-car ferry transports vacationers across the quarter-mile harbor to an isthmus the retreat calls home. The Inn, with 33 rooms on three floors, opened in 1929 when the town was known as "sin city" and visitors came to dance, gamble, and drink. The Resort, its more modern sister, was built in 2007 and sits across the street. Its 11 oceanview suites are more polished than the original hotel.

The Resort's Mediterranean architecture houses guest rooms with Italian marble floors, zebrawood, and sofas strewn with faux fur pillows. Dogs up to 75 pounds can visit the European enclave with a $50 fee the first night and $25 on subsequent evenings. The adjacent Peninsula Park and a three-mile beachside boardwalk supply plenty of freedom for pups to exercise. Pooches are not

allowed at the pool, but they're free to amble around the remaining property, including the second floor patio where Continental breakfast is served daily from 7 a.m. to 10 a.m.

The Inn's Siena Restaurant courtyard is reminiscent of a small Italian coastal village, where dogs nap tableside as guests dine on Zuppa Del Giorno, Chicken Piccata, and the fresh catch of the day. Nothing highfalutin, just a casual lunch or sunset dinner. Prefer a more private venue? Twenty-four-hour room service is delivered to any of the outside nooks among the resort's guest rooms. Here you can listen to seabirds sing while sipping merlot and watching the Pacific waves crash.

FAIRMONT NEWPORT BEACH

4500 MacArthur Boulevard, Newport Beach, CA 92660
(800) 810-3039 • (949) 476-2001
www.fairmont.com/newportbeach ($$)
....

Pet-toting travelers with an early morning flight can tack on an extra day of vacation with an overnight at this property near John Wayne airport. It's located five miles inland among the plethora of O.C. office complexes. The Air France flight crew lay over at the high-rise, so brush up on your *francais* if you want to socialize with them.

After purchasing the hotel in 2005, the Fairmont plunked $32 million into a complete renewal, resulting in a Four Diamond beauty with dark British Colonial woods and buttery leathers. All 440 rooms on the 10 floors are pet-friendly for a $25 per day fee and a maximum size of 30 pounds. Bowls, bed, and nutritional cookies from Three Dog Bakery make pooches feel right at home.

Mealtime is a bit precarious, given there's only one place to dine in the hotel, Bambu Restaurant & Lounge, and it's off-limits to pets. Although not official, the adjacent hallway – which one bellman coined "The Bambu Corridor" – suffices as a pseudo-eatery, with cushy chairs and diminutive side tables for folks dining with pets. Those wanting to eat elsewhere can pick up a list of 15 pooch-permitting nearby restaurants from the concierge. A complimentary shuttle will chauffeur two and four-legged guests within a two-mile radius. The driver also offers 24 hour transport to quaint Balboa Island and Fashion Island open-air shopping center, both great day outings.

WYNDHAM ORANGE COUNTY

3350 Avenue of the Arts , Costa Mesa, CA 92626

(714) 751-5100 • www.wyndham.com ($)

....

The Wyndham's General Manager, Thomas Smalley, is an avid animal lover and an instrumental member of Greyhound Pets of America. His affinity shows in the "Paws and Claws" package. A Pet Care Manager contacts guests prior to arrival to review Fido's amenities and offer a check-list of necessities. Food bowls, dog bed,

bottled water and a choice of rawhide chews, Milk Bones, or dog cookies are included on the roster. With this kind of thoughtfulness, visitors can overlook the guest rooms' need for an update. A 75 pound weight limit ensures almost any dog can visit. Five dollars per room, per night from the package is donated to Smalley's beloved organization.

Every day from 4 p.m. to 7 p.m., the hotel's restaurant, TerraNova, hosts Yappy Hour on the patio overlooking a manmade lake surrounded by lush lawns and nearby high-rise condos. The Paws and Claws Buffet Breakfast on Saturdays and Sundays allows dogs to eat off pet china and lap "Sauvignon Bark" or "Barkundy" alcohol-free beef au jus. An accompanying Bubbles and Bones Champagne bar is worth the extra fee. One dollar of each meal goes to GPA.

Theater and art enthusiasts will be thrilled with the hotel's proximity to Costa Mesa's cultural district. Five performing arts venues, including the Orange County Performing Arts Center, South Coast Repertory, and Segerstrom Concert Hall are within walking distance. The hotel will arrange pet-sitting. Should you want to book ahead of time, e-mail petrequest@wyndham.com .

THE WESTIN SOUTH COAST PLAZA
686 Anton Boulevard, Costa Mesa, CA 92626
(714) 540-2500 • www.westin.com ($)

....

This Westin is within a dozen miles or less from everything in Orange County. Balboa Island, 11 miles. Laguna, 10 miles. The beach, 8 miles. Fashion Island, 5 miles. The hotel caters to a health-conscious clientele with its full fitness center and superfood nutritious meals on the menu.

As with all Westins, pups stay for free and should be 40 pounds or less, but the staff turns a blind eye to larger canine chums. The three-page Dog Waiver at check-in seems overkill in comparison to the hotel's relaxed attitude. Guest rooms have matching Heavenly Beds.

Fifi's is an oversized pillow designed by Eloise Pet Accessories, whose celebrity followers include Debra Messing and Daryl Hannah. Waste bags and a Westin collar tag, with space to write your cell phone number, are provided. In-room spa treatments and meal service assure must-have vacationing comforts.

The lobby lounge merits a stop. Light fare, cocktails and flat-screen TV's make it popular with guests and O.C. residents to watch sports. Waterfall Terrace is a more serene option, with its cascading ten-foot stream and sunshine.

HILTON WATERFRONT BEACH RESORT

21100 Pacific Coast Highway, Huntington Beach, CA 92648 🐕🐕🐕🐕

(714) 845-8000 • (800) 822-7873

www.waterfrontbeachresort.hilton.com ($$)

....

The Hilton's two-mile proximity to Huntington Beach Dog Beach makes it a "must stay" for Fido and friends. All 290 rooms grant privileges to pooches 75 pounds or less for 75 bones per stay. Management has gone the extra mile with a "Wag It at the Waterfront" insignia on dog bowls and beds. A provided dog hanger reads "Travel is more than just A to B. Travel should celebrate your best friend." The resort has partnered with Preservation Society of Huntington Dog Beach. To date, Hilton has donated a vehicle to the organization, along with numerous man-hours of volunteer time.

"It's A Wonderful Dog's Life" package is all about the mutt. A keepsake food bowl, two Dog Beach sweatshirts, brochures on pet-sitting services and a 20-minute walk by the bellman round out the indulgence. Five dollars of the package price is donated to PSof-HDB. Dogs are permitted poolside, but no swimming. Bike rentals are available with baskets for lapdogs, and pull-behind trailers for larger K9s.

Few, if any, Four Diamond hotels showcase pooch pics on the wall of their restaurant, but the Surf Hero Deli does. The Wall of Woof proudly displays photos of employees' scruffy best friends. "Brit," the hotel manager's Yellow Lab, is framed wearing shades; "Skipper," the chef's Weimaraner, is rollicking on the beach, and the catering manager's Dachshund, "Murphy," is hanging out. An adjacent wall mural depicts pups gleefully playing on the beach. Fruity cocktails named "Tail Wagger" and "Dog Whisperer" accompany the light fare at the casually cool café.

THE SHOREBREAK HOTEL

500 Pacific Coast Highway, Huntington Beach, CA 92648
(714) 861-4470 • www.shorebreakhotel.com ($$)
....

Cowabunga dude, this surf-theme hotel is way cool! The new kid on the block opened in the summer of 2009 to rave reviews. Settled in one block from Main Street along the Pacific Coast Highway, this 157 room boutique hotel is in the heart of the action. The masterminds of the property wanted a destination that was sporty, relaxed, connected, and edgy; they got it all with Shorebreak.

Dogs up to 50 pounds can hang-ten for free at Sbk, as it's referred to in-house. Guest rooms have monogrammed pet beds with faux-mink tops and natural puppy pastries in the shape of surfboards. A Pet Butler will arrange walks, sitting, and grooming after a day at Dog Beach.

When checking in, catch a glimpse of the surfing videos shown on the lobby wall 24/7. Surrounding walls are adorned with retro-1960s snapshots from Surf Magazine's photographer, Ron Stoner, and art pieces from John Van Hamersveld of Beatles and Rolling Stone album cover fame. The entryway has a lockable surfboard rack for those who bring their own "sticks," as the wave riders call them.

The hotel's Zimzula restaurant got its name from Riptionary, a surf lingo website. It means "free-spirited person who finds peace with the sand between their toes." Diners find peace with the mouthwatering Moroccan Chicken Tagine and the Mezze Plate comprised of hummus, cauliflower salad with "harissa" – a blend of spices – and feta cheese with basil leaves. Top it off with one of the many drink selections and you have a divine evening. Dining dogs can join owners on the outside balcony deck, which sports stellar views of the Huntington Beach Pier and the Pacific beyond.

Kibble

TRADITION BY PASCAL
Pascal Epicerie & Wine Shop, 1000 North Bristol Street
Newport Beach, CA 92660
(949) 263-9400 • www.pascalnewportbeach.com ($$$$)
....

Step across Pascal's threshold and you've time-traveled to France. *Pain au chocolate* (pastry with chocolate), pates, Cornichon pickles, and Salad Nicoises with poached salmon are the tip of the culinary iceberg. Chef Pascal Olhats has been a pivotal figure on the Newport restaurant scene since 1988. His eateries have been rated number one in Orange County for more than ten years. The shopping center location is low-key, but the breakfast, lunch, and dinner cuisine is top-notch, serving such European delicacies as Escargot with Toasted Pine Nuts and Garlic Butter. The restaurant and upscale deli sit side-by-side with outdoor tables for

you and your furry *chien*. Pascal's joie de vivre atmosphere extends invitations for patrons to join the owner on a cruise through Italy, France, and Monaco to learn culinary techniques.

AMELIA'S ON BALBOA ISLAND

311 Marine Avenue, Balboa Island, CA 92622
(949) 673-6580 • www.ameliasbalboaisland.com ($$)

Founder Amelia Seton, a native Italian, started cooking marinara sauce here in 1961, making this the oldest family-owned and operated restaurant in Orange County. Over the years, it has been the epicenter of countless reunions, birthdays, and wedding events. While the number-one seller is a Filet Mignon/Scampi combo, the linguini, parmigiana, cannelloni, and fresh fish should not be overlooked. Seton's daughter and son-in-law have taken the helm, perpetuating the same great lunches and dinners customers have come to love. The Balboa Island eatery has a sweet, tiny patio peeking out from behind an ornate wrought-iron gate at the entrance. Its one outdoor table sits on a mosaic tile terrace surrounded by potted plants, making it ideal for small to medium dogs.

BASILIC RESTAURANT

217 Marine Avenue, Balboa Island, CA 92662
(949) 673-0570 • www.basilicrestaurant.com ($$$)

Swiss-born chef Bernard Althaus cooks dishes from his home country praiseworthy of Zagat's top restaurant list. The cozy, dinner-only spot looks like a dark-wood chalet in the alps. As with the majority of Balboa Island's eateries, Basilic's snug size dictates only one table on the front patio, with just enough room for pups to curl up in the corner. The first Tuesday of the winter months

is "Raclette Night," a cheese fondue from the Canton of Valais in Switzerland. It is prepared by holding the imported, flavorful Swiss cheese close to a fire, and as it melts, scraping the soft part off to savor with bread, potatoes, or directly into your mouth. Other evenings, Chef Bernard wows guests with Orange Soy Glazed Scallops and Shrimp, Coq au Vin, and Rack of Lamb. The place fills up quickly, so reservations are recommended.

PAS.TU RESTAURANT
216 Marine Avenue, Balboa Island, CA 92622
(949) 566-9525 • www.pasturestaurant.com ($$$)
....

Pas.tu is diminutive in size, but not in taste. One table sits on the front sidewalk of this classy Balboa Island establishment, inviting pooches and people to sit and enjoy its French Mediterranean cuisine. Ivy and pansies overflow from a flower box attached to the entryway's wrought-iron façade. The lunch and dinner menus are divided into Land Plates, Ocean Plates and Pasta Plates, featuring specialties such as Rabbit Stew with Burgundy Sauce, Bouillabaisse and Linguini Gamberetti with Marinara Sauce. The wine selection is a trip around the world with varietals from Europe, South America, and the United States.

SPRINKLES CUPCAKES
Corona Del Mar Plaza
944 Avocado Avenue, Newport Beach, CA 92660
(949) 760-0003 • www.sprinklescupcakes.com ($)
....

These aren't your mother's cupcakes; Sprinkles has made the scrumptious little orbs cool. A husband and wife team runs the mega-popular confectionary which has grown to six locations in OC, with more in the works. Obscure flavors of chai latte or chocolate marshmallow are delicious, but red velvet is by far the favorite. Fans stand in line to purchase boxes of the tasty cakes. Others order online to pick up. Three-tiered cupcake towers are festive for parties. Cupcakes are made fresh daily and leftovers are donated to local

foodbanks. Any of the twenty-two flavors are sure to please, so go ahead, splurge... you're on vacation.

SPARK WOODFIRE GRILL

300 Pacific Coast Highway, Suite 202, Huntington Beach, CA 92648
(714) 960-0996 • www.sparkwoodfiregrill.com ($$$)

Bon Appetit magazine selected Spark Woodfire Grill as one of the "Best Neighborhood Restaurants in the country." Big honor for a beach town of only 200,000 residents. The second-floor eatery off bustling Main Street is open for dinner only. A heated terrace with fire pits makes alfresco dining comfortable for pups and people after the sun sets. Their woodfire hickory grill and 1600-degree broiler are the secret to succulent jumbo prawns and juicy filet

mignon. It's a toss-up whether the Slow-Cooked Baby-Back Ribs, Herb Crusted Halibut, the bar's selection of 50 specialty martinis, or the ocean view have kept patrons returning since 2002. Probably all of the above.

KOKOMO'S SURFSIDE GRILL
21071 Pacific Coast Highway/First Street @ lifeguard tower #5
(lower level on beach), Huntington Beach, CA 92648
(714) 374-5600

PARK BENCH CAFÉ
17732 Goldenwest Street, Huntington Beach, CA 92648
(714) 842-0775 • www.parkbeachcafe.com ($$ both)
....

The owners of these two restaurants, Mike and Christie Bartusick, are superstars in the dog world. In 1993, they created the first Canine Cuisine menu in the U.S.A., catching the attention of television crews from Animal Planet, Travel Channel and E!. Hungry hounds flip for the best-selling Hot Diggity Dog, an all-beef wiener

minus the bun, as well as 11 other selections such as Rover Easy scrambled eggs. Kokomo Grill's surfside location is more than a beach concession stand. It's a family-run eatery

where mom, grandma, kids, cousins, and nephews serve home-made lunches and heaping breakfast plates. Their hours fluctuate, depending on the season. Three miles east is Park Bench Café, nestled among the towering trees of Central Park's 350-acres. Countless fans visit regularly, like Standard Poodles "Josie" and "Sammy," who stop by every Thursday. Weekends can see 50 dogs come and go in a day.

Play

NEWPORT AT YOUR FEET

Private Custom Tours, Newport Beach. CA

(949) 285-7558 • www.newportatyourfeet.com ($$)

....

Carolyn Clark has been conducting foot tours of Newport Beach and beyond since 2004. She is a delightful woman who communicates with ease. Her litany of professional credentials includes a long stint at Walt Disney World in Orlando. Clark caters to visitor's every whim with customized itineraries or pre-planned gadabouts running from three hours up to a full day. Tours of Los Angeles, Beverly Hills, and Hollywood are offered, but Balboa Island and the environs are near and dear to her heart, as she is a resident of the community. Bowser can tag along on numerous outings; just inform Clark beforehand. A luxury limo transports pups and people from the hotel to a designated location where she launches the outing and regales guests with local trivia and historic facts.

DUFFY ELECTRIC BOAT COMPANY

2001 West Coast Highway, Newport Beach, CA 92663

(949) 645-6812 • www.duffyofnewportbeach.com ($$$$)

....

Ahoy, mate! No visit to Newport Beach is complete without a jaunt around the harbor in a Duffy boat. The electric-powered cruiser was invented by a local man, Marshall "Duffy" Duffield, in 1970 when he replaced his small boat's gas tank with a golf cart motor. Almost four decades and over 3,000 boats later, Duffy Boats are synonymous with the O.C. waterways. A canopy and "izing glass" – a thick, clear plastic that doesn't get milky – encloses the 11-passenger, emission-free nautical toy, making it available for year-round trolling. Food and beverages are permitted onboard. Bring your own tunes for the CD player. Dogs 50 pounds or less can join the party free of charge. Rental hours are noon to 8 p.m. weekdays, and till 10 p.m. on weekends.

GOLDENROD FOOTBRIDGE
West on Goldenrod Avenue until dead-ends at bridge
Corona Del Mar, CA 92625
(949) 673-4050 (Corona Del Mar Chamber of Commerce)
www.cdmchamber.com • www.ocdailyphoto.com
....

Situated in a quaint, upscale neighborhood, this overpass was built in 1928 for $10,884, providing convenient access across the "Pacific Gulch" to the beach. At the time of construction, only 2,000 residents called Corona Del Mar home. Today, the 243-foot bridge lined with hot pink geraniums continues to transport people to the Newport Channel promenade and Lookout Point three blocks west. The gulch is now a pocket park and playground, approachable by 51 stairs, where canines and kids can frolic. On the east side of the skywalk is Corona Del Mar village, with boutique shops and bistros.

CRYSTAL COVE STATE PARK
Crystal Cove State Park Historic District & Beach Cottages
Parking lot on east side of Pacific Coast Highway and
Los Trancos intersection, Newport Beach, CA 92657
(949) 497-0900 • (949) 376-6200
www.crystalcovebeachcottages.org • www.crystalcovealliance.org
....

Along the beach of Crystal Cove State Park is the Crystal Cove Historic District, with 46 cottages dating back to the 1920s. Accessible by a pedestrian tunnel under Pacific Coast Highway, this sleepy community depicts the slower SoCal of yesteryear. Originally constructed

as a movie set, and later a summer retreat for countless families, the state acknowledged the Cove's importance in 1979 by placing it on the National Register of Historic Places. The Crystal Cove Alliance, a non-profit organization, has restored 22 of the initial structures to their 1935/1955 condition. Hounds and humans may hike the enclave's miles of seaside paved paths, cool off with one of the Shake Shake's milky concoctions, and browse the quaint gift shop.

DISNEYLAND PARK
Mickey and Friends Parking Structure
1313 South Disneyland Drive, Anaheim, CA 92802
(714) 781-4565
www.disneyland.com ($$ Kennels, $$$$ Disneyland)

If traveling with children, Disneyland is at the top of the list. Indoor kennel facilities for the "Pluto" in your family are located at the main entrance of the theme park. Orange County requires

rabies, distemper, and hepatitis vaccination certificates from a veterinarian, and a minimum pup age of four months. A daily fee of $20 is charged. Not bad, for The Happiest Place On Earth.

DOGGIE BUS

Laurel Glen Park, 13301 Myford Road, Tustin, CA 92780

(714) 906-354 • Cbrixen@cox.net • www.doggiebus.com

....

Who let the dogs out? Corey Brixen did when he purchased a Ford
Econoline bus in December 2007 to shuttle pets and their people to
Huntington Beach Dog Beach. This fun-loving guy removed half
the seats, allowing him to transport 12 mutts and a few less masters.
He installed a 37" flat screen TV to show dog movies and wrapped
the outside with photos of his Jack Russells. Brixen then announced
free round-trip

rides from a Tustin
park 18 miles
inland to the pooch
playground. Before
long he and his
four pups – Josie,
Jonny, Jackson, and
Archie – were
hosting Sunday
treks. It's not a
business; Brixen
owns a screen
printing company
which keeps him busy Monday through Friday. The three-hour
outing on the Doggie Bus is strictly for fun. Brixen cleans, fuels,
and maintains it with his own moola. Appreciative passengers
attempt to donate money, but the dog-lover won't accept. Since its
inception there have been no altercations, just tail-waggin' good
times. Eager participants check out the website or phone Brixen
for weekly updates. Without a doubt, this pleasure trip is a must-do
when in Huntington Beach.

HUNTINGTON BEACH DOG BEACH (HBDB)

Pacific Coast Highway, between Goldenwest Street and
Seapoint Street, Huntington Beach, CA 92648

(714) 841-8644 • www.dogbeach.org

....

Touted as one of the most popular dog beaches in the United
States, this one-mile strip of sand is pure unadulterated fun. Plenty

of nearby parking is available. A tall seawall protects playing pups from the street. Surfers and swimmers can catch a wave alongside their doggie-paddling pooches. Purina Dog Chow and the Hilton Waterfront Beach Resort have donated and installed three canine drinking fountains. Volunteers meticulously maintain the leash-free area, placing ten trash bins and three biodegradable waste-bag stations intermittently along the shore. The dedicated group has been recognized by Disney for its service to the dog beach. Apparel adorned with the HBDG canine cartoon logo is sold on their website, with proceeds benefiting the upkeep of the pooch paradise.

DIG IT! SAND CASTLES
(714) 206-2877 • www.digitsandcastles.blogspot.com
www.africano.org ($$$$)
....

Marc and Michelle Africano love playing in the sand. So much so, that four years ago the husband and wife duo started a business on how to construct the perfect sand castle, complete with turrets and a moat. It's an opportunity for families, corporate groups, or just couples and their hole-diggin' hounds to grab their inner child and spend time together. Wanna-be castellans are given the choice of numerous meeting spots, including dog beach. A three-hour minimum is usually needed to bring the castle of your dreams to fruition. The Africanos charge per hour and provide shovels, troughs, carving tools, buckets, and other necessities, as well as their expertise. Building sessions are seven days a week in the summer, but the seaside architects are both school teachers, so September through May is on weekends, and weekdays after three.

Fetch

BALBOA ISLAND
Newport Beach, CA 92662
www.balboa-island.com • www.balboa-island.net
www.zschoche.com

....

This is the "Mayberry RFD" of Southern California, where residents say hello and bicycles are the preferred mode of transportation. Flower boxes and American flags decorate the wood-shingled cottages. Mature trees canopy two-lane streets and park benches

dot the sidewalks, inviting visitors to sit and watch the world go by. Marine Avenue anchors the three-block shopping district of this 2.5-square mile island in Newport Bay. A bridge connects it to the mainland. The friendly warmth of family-owned shops and restaurants makes customers feel like guests. There are no chain stores, and locals were aghast when Starbucks made it onto their peaceful hamlet. Masters and mutts should mosey into Zschoche to catch the most current lifestyle items, such as retro Pan Am airline bags, and Eco Sneakers made of recycled products. A few doors down is Island Home, a mother and daughter-owned boutique selling frills for the home. The owner of Aloha Balboa Antiques lived in Kauai for 20 years, and has an eye for impeccable vintage Hawaiian estate jewelry and prints from the 1940s and 50s. They were voted "Best Antiques in Orange County" by OC Magazine.

FASHION ISLAND
401 Newport Center Drive, Newport Beach, CA 92660
(800) 495-4753 • (949) 721-2000
www.shopfashionisland.com • www.cafebeausoleil.net
www.ilfornaio.com

This outdoor mall is so O.C. with towering palms, a Koi pond complete with bamboo trees and meditative benches, and views

of the glistening Pacific beyond. Nearly 200 stores — including biggies Nordies, Neimans and Bloomies — entertain shoppers for hours, if not days. It's not unusual to see a French Bulldog or handsome Golden Retriever accompany its parents on a spree. Juicy Couture sells pink pet carriers and leashes reading Fetch Couture. A Betsey Johnson boutique treats pups to water and doggie snaps. Bloomingdale's 59th and Lex Café's stylish crowd includes those with paws, as does Café Beau Soleil and Canaletto Ristorante Veneto.

BELLA TERRA MALL
7777 Edinger Avenue, Huntington Beach, CA 92647
(714) 897-2534 • www.bellaterra-hb.com

Huntington is extremely laid-back, and the shopping venues mimic the coastal-casual mindset. Terra Bella has the fanciest stores this beach town offers. When catering to a population that lives in board shorts and flip-flops, there is no need for anything more than REI and Diane's Beachwear. Cost Plus World Market adds a bohemian flair to the alfresco mall. Bargain hunters share Tacone Gourmet Wraps and Island Fish Tacos with their scruffy sidekicks on the numerous umbrella-shaded chairs around the plaza.

Veterinarian

COSTA MESA ANIMAL HOSPITAL
480 East 17th Street, Costa Mesa, CA 92627
(949) 548-3794 • www.costamesaanimalhospital.com
Offers 24 hour, seven days a week, on-call emergency service.

Not Carnegie, Vanderbilt and Astor together could have raised
money enough to buy a quarter share in my little dog.
– Ernest Thompson Seton

Los Angeles is humongous. To drive from the northern border on the Tejon Pass to the south county line at Long Beach takes two hours. Ten million people call this sprawling parcel home. Its 88 cities are a melting pot of ethnic cultures and American eras. L.A.'s Chinatown is the second largest in California, after San Francisco. Filipinotown, Hollywood and Beverly Hills coexist within a twelve-mile radius, and the historic 1930s Farmers Market shares Fairfax Avenue with avant-garde CBS Studios. The paparazzi buzz around the city snapping photos of dog-toting celebrities going about day-to-day life. Movie stars' trendsetting tendency has made it cool to hang with your pooch, spurring hotels and bistros to be more lenient with their pet policies. Even LAX Airport is Fido-friendly. A small "pet park" is located at the southeast end of the Central Terminal near United Airlines Terminal 7-8, complete with a dog house and bio-bags. That's good news for vacationing pups. The entertainment capital is waiting, so seize all it has to offer!

LOS ANGELES

LONG BEACH • PALOS VERDES • MARINA DEL REY

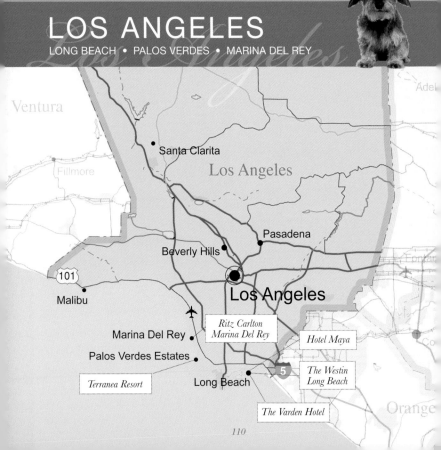

Stay

THE WESTIN LONG BEACH

333 East Ocean Boulevard, Long Beach, CA 90802
(562) 436-3000 • www.westin.com ($$)

....

True story…a couple traveled throughout Asia for three weeks. Upon arriving in Kyoto, Japan, they stayed one night at the Westin Miyako, complete with the hotel's signature Heavenly Bed and massage treatments. The experience was so indelible it left the couple to coin the phrase, "Remember the Westin?", followed by a long sigh whenever they stay at a less-than-perfect inn. It is this kind of lure the Westin has on its guests, and the Long Beach property is no exception.

It's classy without trying too hard. Management realizes a paw print or two could smudge the vestibule's marble floor, but pets are unequivocally part of the family and are as welcome as two-legged members. A Heavenly Dog Bed and bowls ensure creature comforts, all free of charge. A 40 pound weight limit is suggested but not enforced.

People and pooches can resuscitate their tired bodies at the lobby lounge's nightly gathering dubbed, "unwind." Cocktails and cuisine are served among candle-light and soft music. Should you desire a meal with more sustenance, The Grill restaurant's outside patio will satiate anyone's hunger pang.

An evening stroll is the ideal nightcap, given the hotel's downtown, harbor-view location. The front desk staff will provide area maps to navigate Long Beach's burgeoning metropolis. Runner's World magazine created a three-and-five-mile jogging route for those who want to pick up the pace. Pocket-size, laminated diagrams are available. So when only the best will do, remember the Westin.

HOTEL MAYA

700 Queensway Drive, Long Beach, CA 90802
(562) 453-3669 • (562) 453-3675
www.hotelmayalongbeach.com ($$)

....

This exotic Latin American hotel lounges on Long Beach's south waterfront on its picturesque rocky coast, sharing a spit of land with the majestic Queen Mary and Carnival cruise terminal. Views of the downtown skyline across Queensway Bay are unsurpassed, and for that alone warrant a visit.

The resort's chartreuse and white buildings sprout like wildflowers among the verdant landscape. Funky guest rooms with parrot-green shutters, river-rock headboards, and tangerine lamps sound zany, but somehow work well together. Ground floor rooms grant pooches easy access to sprawling lawns. Coddled critters, big or small, pay *nada* to stay here. Sunbathers and their domesticated dependents can loaf poolside, but remember, only the two-legged type are allowed in the water.

Fuego Restaurant features coastal Mexican cuisine. Chef Jesse Perez whips up delicious Limon Jamon Serrano and Cilantro Jalapeno Steak Tacos. *Gringos* may want the milder White Corn Sopes. Cool down the tongue with a Hibiscus Lemonade Rickey — Bombay gin, tea, lemon and soda. Finish up with a shot of Latin nectar from the bar's largest selection of tequila in the region. Pets aren't permitted at the restaurant, but the same great food and drinks can be enjoyed on the lobby's outdoor esplanade.

THE VARDEN HOTEL
335 Pacific Avenue, Long Beach, CA 90802
(877) 3VARDEN (382-7336) • (562) 432-8950
www.thevardenhotel.com ($)
....

The Varden has a higher percentage of urban cool than it has opulence. There is no valet parking or room service. What they do have is a 1929 hotel with a wacky history, that has been morphed into a 35 room uber-contemporary boutique European inn. During the Depression, a wealthy man bought the hotel for his circus performer mistress, Dolly Varden, hence the present-day name. The ensuing 80 years saw the structure fall into disrepair until its purchase and extensive renovation one year ago. The original construction shows behind the white paint covering every surface. An occasional spot of color can be found in the bluish-gray

hallway and guest room carpet. Kudos are in order for maintaining the integrity of the round-penny tile, which the construction crew unearthed in the bathrooms beneath six inches of concrete.

Those with wet noses and wagging tails are met with open arms by the staff. The owners mumble something about a weight restriction of 25 pounds, but everyone knows a Standard Poodle, who shall remain nameless, frequents the property as well as Lady Ashley, the proprietor's English Bulldog. The main objective is for pooches to be well behaved. A $50 cleaning fee per stay is enforced.

A complimentary continental breakfast is served in the upper living room off the lobby until 9 a.m.. Dogs are welcome if you can pry Fido off the Simmons plush pillow-top mattress. Afternoon wine-tasting and snacks lure guests back from a day of sightseeing. The hotel is located in one of Long Beach's up-and-coming areas, with the emphasis on "coming." Pine Avenue, The Pike, Shoreline Village, and beaches are all within walking distance making it the ideal way for you and your critter to see the city *au pied*.

TERRANEA RESORT
6610 Palos Verdes Drive South, Palos Verdes, CA 90275
(310) 265-2800 • www.terranea.com ($$$)
....

The name Terranea is derived from the hotel's signature Medi"terranea"n architecture and pronounced ter-a-NAY-a. Its 102-acres are terraced flawlessly into a hillside overlooking the Pacific Ocean. The property nuzzles a protected habitat, so certain environmental measures must be taken, including the filtration of rain runoff before it reaches the sea. The three swimming pools

are treated with salt in lieu of chlorine.

Television buffs may recognize the location from the popular 1950s show, *Sea Hunt*, where 155 episodes were filmed. Marineland of the Pacific, a seaside animal theme park, called the isthmus home for 32 years prior to Terranea's inception. Forty-five trees from the oceanarium were salvaged and replanted throughout the resort.

The 582 guest quarters are comprised of rooms, suites, and bungalows. Ground floor rooms are reserved for those traveling with pooches. The ratio of a $150 pet fee to the darling's limited access seems misskewed. There is no weight limit; however, there are breed restrictions that ban Rottweilers, Doberman Pinschers, Chow Chows, Akitas, and Pit Bulls from the hotel.

Art displayed throughout the resort was created by members of the Portuguese Bend Artist Colony, named after the peninsula's remaining undeveloped land. The group of seven childhood friends who grew up in the area are dedicated to stimulating conservation awareness and capturing the raw beauty through their paintings as a record for future generations.

The aforementioned habitat is best seen on the resort's bluff-top Discovery Trail. Pooches and people wind along coastal sage scrub, nesting birds, and above ocean crags harboring frothy waves below. Glimpses may be caught of Donald Trump's public golf course three miles south.

There are four options for dining dogs. Nelson's, named after *Sea*

Hunt's main character, Mike Nelson, overlooks the cove where the series was shot. Benches surround a fire ring where servers are happy to deliver the pub's fare. From May until September picnic tables at Discovery Trail Refreshments provide salty snacks, a low water fountain for parched pups, and stellar sunrises and sunsets. The adjacent Cielo pool restricts pets, but visitors can order from the café's menu to enjoy at the trail's outdoor tables. The lobby terrace lets pups accompany parents for coffee and cocktails. Hotel pet sitters are not available, which means room service is the other option.

RITZ-CARLTON MARINA DEL REY
4375 Admiralty Way, Marina Del Rey, CA 90292
(310) 823-1700 • www.ritzcarlton.com ($$$)
....

Ritz-Carlton hotels are synonymous with luxury, and the Marina del Rey property is no exception. The 14-story monolith resides in L.A.'s trendy Westside, beside the largest recreational marina in the country. Just five miles north of LAX Airport, this waterfront beauty can be an overnight stop for those traveling to far-flung destinations, or a weekend pardon from day-to-day life. Its proximity to beach communities and the hinterlands makes it more desirable than remote resort choices.

The J. Paul Getty museums, Dodger Stadium and the Lakers' Staples Center are all within twenty miles of the Five Diamond hotel. A canine caretaker via the concierge makes it possible to leave the pooch in good hands while enjoying the City of Angels. All 304 guest rooms indulge furry friends 30 pounds or less. Portfolios are charged $125.

The dog-sitter will come in handy if dining at any of the hotel's three restaurants, or using the state-of-the-art fitness center and spa, as these cater to people only. One eating option with petable patrons is benches on a promenade running along the harbor. Souvenir coolers filled with goodies are available from room service. Choose from The Marina — salads, sandwiches and snacks, or The Hollywood — which includes the same, plus a fact kit and guide to celebrity points of interests. Evening meals can be savored in-room while swaddled in a soft robe and slippers.

Kibble

PARKER'S LIGHTHOUSE

435 Shoreline Village Drive, Long Beach, CA 90802
(562) 432-6500 • www.parkerslighthouse.com ($$$)
....

Parker's is on the San Pedro Bay waterfront among the shops and cafes of Shoreline Village. Their 144-seat deck, with glass walls to barricade cool ocean breezes, imparts views of the Queen Mary

and fishing boats scooting across the water. The corner location is devoid of loud crowds and doesn't impinge on canines catching a few winks while their parents eat. A handful of beef, pork, and chicken dishes are listed on the menu, but the shellfish and seafood delicacies put the Long Beach favorite on L.A.'s "Top Five Seafood Restaurants" list.

SALUZZI RISTORANTE D'ITALIA
31206 Palos Verdes Drive West, Rancho Palos Verdes, CA 90275
(310) 377-7200 • www.saluzzis.com ($$$)
....

With newspaper accolades saying "a culinary gem" and "to die for," Palos Verdes vacationers would be remiss to let this dining

opportunity pass. Award-winning, Four Star chef Michael Saluzzi, and his brother Joseph have brought their Old World Italian cooking to the peninsula. A 40-seat patio is the epicenter for pet-toting patrons. The lunch menu's Shrimp and Tangy Parmigiana Cheese Sandwich along with a Lobster and Cracked Crab Salad is their incentive. Dinners are equally scrumptious. The Mushroom-Stuffed Gnocchi runs a close second to the Conch With Roasted Garlic Creamed Polenta.

ORGANIC PANIFICIO CAFE
4211 Admiralty Way, Marina Del Rey, CA 90292
(310) 448-8900 ($$)
....

The view alone is worth the visit. A deck overlooking the harbor and its armada of pleasure crafts is enough to make mutts and masters drool. Fresh, organic Italian food is the house specialty. Homemade "from scratch" pizzas, pastas, and salads complement the great location. Weekend breakfasts dole out fluffy omelets to a sizeable crowd, and the evenings serve up DJ tunes to dance the night away.

THE GONDOLA GETAWAY

5437 East Ocean Boulevard, Long Beach, CA 90803

(562) 433-9595 • www.gondo.net ($$$)

....

Oh solo mio isn't an issue at this pet-friendly gondola company. No need to ride alone when you can bring along a canine chum for free. Authentic Venetian boats glide through the peaceful canals of Naples Island, powered by the arms of young bucks dressed as Italian gondoliers. Multi-million-dollar homes with yachts tethered to their private docks line the waterways. Fifty-minute tours are offered from 11a.m. until 11p.m. seven days a week, equipped with a complimentary basket of cheese and crackers, wine glasses, and ice bucket. Otherwise it's BYOB. Eva Longoria and Tony Parker, among other celebrities, have been spotted on a romantic cruise. Being the first gondola company in California has its perks.

OFF-LEASH DOG BEACH ZONE

East Ocean Boulevard, between Roycroft Avenue and Argonne Avenue, Long Beach, CA 90803

(800) 452-7829 • (562) 436-3645

(Long Beach Convention and Visitors Bureau)

www.justinrudd.com • www.santapaws.info

www.hautedogs.org • www.visitlongbeach.com

....

The only off-leash dog beach in Los Angeles County rolls out three acres of coastline for furry friends to fly across the sand. The devoted custodian of this sandy plot is Justin Rudd. Few men are more loyal to bettering pets' lives than

this go-getter, who brought the venture to fruition in June 2001. His bulldog, Rosie, was the reason for the family-friendly seaside playground, and his Easter Dog Parade, Howl'oween Parade, and Santa Paws fundraisers. The Beach Zone requests one pooch per person. There is plenty of parking and a doggie water fountain. Hours are 6 a.m. until 8 p.m. seven days a week.

PORTUGUESE BEND
Palos Verdes Drive South, Palos Verdes, CA 90275
(310) 377-8111 • www.palosverdeschamber.com
....

The journey is the destination on this five-mile scenic drive along the coast. Invaluable geological flora and fauna, which aid ecologists' research, can be found along the crooked road with jaw dropping views. Plants endemic to the Channel Islands in the Pacific almost 100 miles north are found here, leaving botanists to believe

the archipelago and the Palos Verdes Peninsula were once one. Sightseers pass the landmark glass Wayfarer Chapel built by Lloyd Wright, son of architect Frank Lloyd Wright. Abalone Cove, Inspiration Point, and Trump International Golf Club are interspersed along the road, as well as stops to walk leashed dogs.

MARINA DEL REY WALKS

Marina Del Rey Visitors Center
4701 Admiralty Way, Marina Del Rey, CA 90292
(310) 305-9545 • www.visitmarinadelrey.com

....

This oceanside basin has numerous self-guided walks for Turf-Pounders or Pleasure-Puppies, whatever your pace. Stroll or march past nesting egrets and great blue herons at the Ballona Wetlands. View thousand of live-aboards, fishing crafts and cruisers at the marina. Rest a spell at Admiralty Park, or take in Pacific breezes on the North Jetty. Step-by-step directions are available on the Visitors' Website or at the Center.

Fetch

4TH STREET RETRO ROW

4th Street, between Temple Avenue and Cherry Avenue
Long Beach, CA 90814
(562) 222-8895 • www.4thstreetlongbeach.com

....

Take a walk on the funky side along this three-block, blast-to-the-past shopping district. Free thinkers spiffied-up the neighborhood, plugged in the 1950s neon signs, and began selling their vintage wares. Forty-three stores and restaurants cater to urban hipsters with Mid-Century clothes and furniture. Xcape peddles antique hard-to-find items. Lil' Devils Boutique

encompasses the entire family with skull-and-crossbone car-seat covers, "Little Buddy" engraved flasks for Dad, and necklaces adorned with a single Scrabble board game tile. Music buffs flock to Open for their local label CD's and vinyl records, as well as the wild art and indie book selection. Grab a bench outside of Number Nine's noodle house and share a Shrimp Egg Roll or Barbequed Pork Sandwich with your pup. Don't forget dessert at Portfolio Coffeehouse.

BELMONT SHORE
East 2nd Street, Long Beach, CA 90803
(562) 434-3066 • www.belmontshore.org
www.bonoslongbeach.com ($$$$)

East Second Avenue is devoted to a charming neighborhood of mostly shops and restaurants. Fifteen blocks of large retailers, owner-operated boutiques and eateries with cuisine spanning the globe sit between the Pacific Ocean on one end and Alamitos Bay on the other. The micro region is popular with the GLBT community, students, families, and young couples with their four-legged "starter child." Strict health codes necessitate mollycoddled fur-kids be tied outside the rail of most restaurant patios. There is one exception – Bono's. A table tucked on the far side of the Italian eatery's terrace allows Fido to share a nibble or two of your Chicken Piccata.

SHORELINE VILLAGE
401-435 Shoreline Village Drive, Long Beach, CA 90802
(562) 435-2668 • www.shorelinevillage.com • www.lids.com

The fifth-largest city in California has been providing family fun for almost three decades at its charming oceanfront harbor with a mishmash of casual cafes, bric-a-brac shops, miles of bike paths, and pocket parks for Fido. It is not chi chi, but the view of the Queen Mary docked across the bay is first class. The architecture replicates a New England port with a wooden boardwalk overlooking the 3,400 slip Shoreline Village Marina. With an average of 345 days of sunshine per year, it behooves travelers to stop by the Village Hat Shop and see the largest selection of "lids" in the world. You may want to rent a scurry afterwards to check out the scenery.

PROMENADE ON THE PENINSULA

550 Deep Valley Drive, Rolling Hills Estates, CA 90274
(310) 541-0688 • www.promenadeonthepeninsula.com
....

The Spanish-style, three-level plaza is an optimum way to exercise the pooch and purchase remembrances of a wonderful vacation. The open-air promenade has only a few dozen shops and cafes, but they're the good ones – Williams-Sonoma, Restoration Hardware, J. Crew, and White House/Black Market. Locals love iBerries with free WiFi to browse the Internet while savoring the creamy delight.

ABBOT KINNEY BOULEVARD

Between Venice Boulevard and Brooks Avenue, Venice, CA 90291
www.abbotkinney.org • www.tortoiselife.com
www.plantationdesign.com • www.abbotshabit.com
www.mariannekooimans.com
....

The neighborhood is named after its 19th century founder, Abbot Kinney, who, after vacationing in Italy, envisioned a Venice of America. Marshy land was transformed into canals with gondola rides, amusement attractions, and flying circuses – the "Coney Island of the Pacific." While Abbot's intention was to create a more sophisticated town, he soon realized the area made a handsome profit and conceded its incarnation. Decades later, the canals are lined with expensive houses, but Venice's beach walk is still filled with peculiar people and souvenir stands.

Abbot Kinney Boulevard has seen a rebirth from head shops and hippies to art galleries, casual restaurants and boutiques. The 80 indie businesses have a bohemian flair, and proprietors are usu-

ally present. Wearable masterpieces of hand-loomed, embroidered textiles fill Koko's store. Tortoise and TGS, both owned by Taku and Keiko Shinomoto, sell Japanese wares for daily living. "Remy," a French Bulldog, chills at Plantation home store, and the scent of brewed java at Abbot's Habit Cafe has replaced the area's once pervasive aroma of patchouli oil.

No matter how little money and how few possessions you own,
having a dog makes you rich.

– Louis Sabin

Veterinarian

ANIMAL EMERGENCY REFERRAL CENTER
3511 Pacific Coast Highway; Suite A, Torrance, CA 90505
(310) 325-3000 • www.aercvet.com
Open 24 hours, seven days a week
....

ASEC
Animal Surgical & Emergency Center
1535 South Sepulveda Boulevard, Los Angeles, CA 90025
24 Hour Emergency (310) 473-1561
Surgery Department (310) 473-5906
www.ASECvets.com
....

Stay

LOEWS SANTA MONICA BEACH HOTEL

1700 Ocean Avenue, Santa Monica, CA 90401

(310) 458-6700 • www.loewshotels.com/santamonica ($$$)

To say Loews loves pets is like claiming the Pacific Ocean is just a pond. This Fido-friendly resort adores pets, and knows how to treat them like rock stars. Big dogs, little dogs, red dogs, yellow dogs… they're all welcome for only 25 bones per stay. Throughout the year, the hotel offers various package deals just for critters. When the Commander-in-Chief's family was seeking a pooch, the "Presidential Pooch" package was available. Employees adorned patriotic pups with Stars-and-Stripes bandanas and served them a feast fit for a king, er, President. Environmentally conscious pups can now enjoy the "Grrrreen Dog" package with a recyclable rubber chew, in-room meal, and an organic cotton bandana. Upon check-in, food bowls, treats, and a placemat to catch messes are delivered to any of the 342 guestrooms.

Loews' 80-foot glass, sun-saturated atrium with indoor palm trees is the hotel's main artery. This is where you'll see haute-hounds coming and going. Guests lollygag here, sipping drinks and meeting fellow hairy heartthrobs.

Pet-sitting is accessible through the concierge, should vacationers want to lounge poolside while taking in views of the Santa Monica Pier. Or make a reservation at Olive and Vine restaurant, yielding an evening of fireside conversation and the house special, "Beach Chowder." Go all-out and stop by Ocean Spa beforehand to transform your tress with Blow hair care products to the stars. Their motto is, "Every woman looks better with a blow out." If there's time, add a few highlights for the total beach look.

SHERATON DELFINA

530 Pico Boulevard, Santa Monica, CA 90405

(310) 399-9344 • www.sheratonsantamonica.com ($$)

....

This Sheraton is hip in a Pottery Barn sort of way. A candle-lit lobby with brunette walls, ornamental coral, and potted orchids is infused with a signature scent called "Open Skies," enhancing the olfactory experience. Upwardly mobile couples and international families frequent the stylish high-rise, positioned five blocks east of the ocean on one of Santa Monica's main thoroughfares.

Cool digs attract cool dogs. Rumor has it that Duke, the Golden Retriever of Bush's Baked Beans fame, stays at the hotel when in town shooting a commercial. The staff will neither confirm or deny, due to celebrity confidentiality. He exceeds the weight limit, which is murky because it's listed as both 40 and 50 pounds. But it doesn't matter; as with all pups, it's not enforced. The $75 pet fee is.

Hounds can hang virtually anywhere in the hotel. The poolside teak deck harbors chaise lounges tempting guests to settle in as canine chums curl up in the shade underneath. Apps, snacks and drinks are served there, as well as at nearby tables and the inside lobby bistro lounge. Huddled beneath the entryway portico is an outside living room with overstuffed sofas and heating lamps for cool evenings. This nook's only duty is to cosset guests as they watch the action on Pico Boulevard, sip the Delfina cocktail of Grey Goose Vanilla, Pama Liquor, Triple Sec and sweet and sour mix, or just chill out.

FAIRMONT MIRAMAR HOTEL & BUNGALOWS
101 Wilshire Boulevard, Santa Monica, CA 90401
(800) 441-1414 • (310) 576-7777
www.fairmont.com/santamonica ($$$$)

....

When entering the filigreed wrought-iron gates, guests are greeted by an eighty-foot Moreton Bay Fig tree planted over 120 years ago and declared a national landmark in 1976. The hotel's three buildings are constructed around the tree, which sits on some of the most valuable real estate in Southern California, overlooking the ocean in the heart of Santa Monica.

The list of celebrity visitors could fill a book. In any given decade since 1921, the retreat has been a Hollywood favorite. Greta Garbo resided here for more than four years, and Betty Grable was "discovered" at the age of 15 while singing at the hotel piano bar. Bill Clinton, Britney Spears, Kobe Bryant and countless others have laid their heads on the goose down pillows.

In November 2008, pups started getting the star treatment when Fairmont launched the P.A.W. (Pets Always Welcome) program. The staff fawns over pups of any size, furnishing a cushy dog bed, squeaky plush toy, bowls, and a box of critter cookies good enough for human consumption. And it's all free. The only requirement is current vaccination records. A pet dining menu includes new zealand venison and v-dog vegetarian nuggets.

Two resident Dachshunds, Cooper and Tucker, can be seen scampering around the property. They live with the Director of Sales and Marketing in one of the 32 bungalows, which have a private enclosed patio, making them ideal for Fido and family. Two high-rises complete the Fairmont's 300 rooms, all surrounded by five acres of lush gardens, waterfalls and paths for peaceful strolls. Just make sure Fido doesn't lift his leg on the priceless sprig out front.

LE MERIGOT
1740 Ocean Avenue, Santa Monica, CA 90401 🐕🐕🐕🐕

(310) 395-9700 • www.LeMerigotHotel.com ($$$)

....

This oceanfront JW Marriott hotel welcomes dogs, cats, birds and fish, should your macaw or beta want to accompany Fido. There is a 100 pound weight restriction and all 175 guestrooms are pet friendly. A $250 deposit is required, with $150 refunded upon checkout if there is no damage to the room.

The pet program was spawned by a former resident Yellow Labrador, Meg. In her honor, the Four Diamond property instigated several creature comforts, including doggie meals served at the signature restaurant, Cezanne, and a delightful gated pooch park with meandering dirt paths and flowering plants. Today, "Baxter," a huge wooden dog wearing a red rhinestone collar, is the pseudo-canine tenant. He stands guard at the concierge desk and is known to turn up by the pool or ride the elevator at times — the result of employee pranks.

A favorite hangout for pups and people is Le Troquet, which means "bar" or "café" in French. On the terrace, it's not unusual to hear locals discuss their friends in the movie industry while sipping ruby red varietals and lime-loaded libations before retiring to Cezanne's nearby patio for dinner.

Make arrangements with the concierge for a pet-sitter and head to the spa for a Caviar and Pearl Lifting Facial, or Chai Soy Mud Wrap. Visits by Brad Pitt and Courtney Cox are a testament to the high quality of service.

For a more active indulgence, professional surfing lessons are offered with the hotel's California Surfin' Safari package. Wet suits and surfboard rentals are included, along with a Swedish massage and Blue Crush martini to round out the experience.

THE GEORGIAN HOTEL

1415 Ocean Avenue, Santa Monica, CA 90401

(800) 538-8147 • (310) 883-6244 • www.GeorgianHotel.com ($$)
....

"Stunning" is the best way to describe this refurbished 1933 Art Deco beauty. The patina façade is wreathed with a gold roof. An inviting front veranda with wrought-iron rails is tucked comfortably under an awning. Ornate plaster crown molding from the hotel's inception circle the foyer ceiling, and elevators from the '30s remain, but have been automated. The original floor-to-ceiling arched windows grant views of Palisades Park and the nearby Santa Monica Pier. "The Lady," as this gem was lovingly nicknamed in the early years, was one of the waterfront's first "skyscrapers," with her eight floors. Today, she's one of many. Once

a getaway for A-listers such as Clark Gable and Carole Lombard, the landmark has maintained the architectural integrity of the early twentieth century, but has updated amenities for the new millennium, with flat-screen televisions, central AC, and complimentary wireless Internet. It's rated 3.5 Stars because there is no pool; otherwise it would be Four Stars.

The 84 guest rooms are decorated from the Art Deco era, with pillbox sofa pillows and large door peepholes fashioned after cruise ship portholes. The bathtub's rubber ducky is a cute touch. Bedtime chocolates and a card with the next day's weather forecast are placed on pillows. Pets up to 50 pounds are welcome. The fee varies; dogs under 25 pounds are charged $100 per stay; larger pups pay $150. Room service is the only dining option for guest with pets in tow, but feel free to enjoy drinks in the lobby living room. Restaurants are within walking distance.

VICEROY SANTA MONICA

1819 Ocean Avenue, Santa Monica, CA 90401

(800) 622-8711 • (310) 260-7500

www.viceroysantamonica.com ($$$)

....

From the outside this hotel looks nondescript, but step through the oversized front door and it's tres fabu! Walls bathed in deep char-

coal are offset with furnishings of white, parrot green, and sunshine yellow. Viceroy's style − created by star designer Kelly Wearstler of Bravo TV's *Top Design* fame − depicts the British Regency period from 1811 to 1820, when lively color became important and wallpaper was a central element.

Any hotel that serves a complimentary glass of champagne upon check-in is a class act. Vacationing pups of any size will feel right at home with the various nods to the animal kingdom throughout this celebrity hangout. The elevator vestibule is flanked by two life-size porcelain Whippets. Greco-Roman Griffins, who have the body of a lion, and head and wings of an eagle embellish the hallways. Guest rooms are equally intriguing. Viceroy's $100 pet fee only includes a dog bowl in the room, so you and the pooch will have to share the bed.

A bright yellow library off the reception area continues the ode to early 19th century color. Books of every genre line the shelves, and a plasma TV beckons visitors to try a hand at Wii bowling. The lobby's leather chaises are another fun place to hang out and try to catch a glimpse of celebrities hiding behind their huge sunglasses.

Pet-sitters will keep Bowser happy for an hour or a day, depending on your budget. Schedule a poolside spa treatment or eat at the hotel restaurant, Whist, named after a British card game. Food + Wine magazine designated it one of "America's 50 best hotel restaurants."

HOTEL CASA DEL MAR

1910 Ocean Way, Santa Monica, CA 90405

(800) 898-6999 • (310) 581-5533 • www.hotelcasadelmar.com ($$$$)

....

This hotel was once a 1920s exclusive beach club for the well-heeled until WWII efforts converted it into military housing. Decades passed and numerous incarnations, including the Pritikin Longevity Center, until a $50 million makeover restored Casa Del Mar to its previous grand luxury status from the flapper era.

The hotel's brick and sandstone façade is a pleasant change from Santa Monica's excess of stucco buildings. Enormous stained-glass doors open to reveal a grand staircase inlaid with custom tile, and an intricately hand-painted ceiling reminiscent of a bygone age.

The guest room's beach-cottage décor is inconsistent with the lobby's opulence, but none the less pleasing. A dark walnut, four-poster bed reigns over the otherwise pastel blue and white motif. It is here that pups spend most of their time, as pooches are prohibited in any public spaces and restaurants. Upon making reservations, guests must "get the OK" from management to bring Fido. There is no charge and pups must be less than 25 pounds. A sitter is available, should guests want to bask poolside, listen to music in the lounge, or retreat to the spa.

Casa's "Wellness Your Way" focuses on incorporating a mental and physical healthy lifestyle into all aspects of your visit. The in-room Wellness Chest provides a complimentary 10,000 Steps walking map, along with other necessary tools to navigate the beach and canyon areas. A preloaded iPod offering tips on optimal gaits is

available at the front desk. For those who need a little push, personal trainers are willing to coerce both two and four-legged couch potatoes out for a simple scenic run. In-room treatments may be the more desired route. A full-body massage de-stresses anyone, or a 25 minute rubdown lying on the room's chaise may be enough. Follow with a whirlpool soak in the bathroom's therapeutic hydra tub. Brain games of Sudoku or Word Scramble given at evening turndown will give equal merit to satisfying the mind. Pleasant dreams.

SHUTTERS ON THE BEACH

One Pico Boulevard, Santa Monica, CA 90405

(800) 334-9000 • (310) 458-0030

www.shuttersonthebeach.com ($$$$)

....

The resort looks like a Hampton's beach house, with soft gray shingled siding trimmed in white, and interior plantation shutters peeking out from the guest rooms. The seaside beauty sits adjacent to its sister property, Casa Del Mar; both are poised perfectly on the promenade that runs along Santa Monica Bay. They are the only hotels in Los Angeles located directly on the sand.

Shutters has the same restrictive pet policy as her sibling next door, except a $125 cleaning fee is tacked onto the bill. Eateries, lounges, lobby and the pool are off limits. Pet-sitting is offered. The Beach

Butler has a good selection of boxed lunches for guests and their sidekicks to enjoy on the boardwalk benches. Room service covers the remaining meals. In an attempt to take the guilt out of snacks, healthy munchies fill the mini-bar, offering Organic Fiji Apple Chips, Think Thin protein bars, Pom Wonderful Juice and all-natural cocktail mixers. These may loosen you up to test the Juggling Balls sitting on the bookshelf. One hour lessons are available for novices. An in-room library subverts any thoughts of exercise, with a selection of novels and coffee table books.

Shutter's personalized concierge service is taken to the next level with "runtriz" technology. Travelers use their iPhone, iPod Touch, Blackberry or laptop to coordinate spa treatments, confirm dinner reservations, contact the Bell Desk, or set wakeup calls. Login information is given upon check-in, making it effortless to be connected.

HUCKLEBERRY CAFÉ AND BAKERY
1014 Wilshire Boulevard, Santa Monica, CA 90404
(310) 451-2311 • www.huckleberrycafe.com ($)
....

A restaurant named Huckleberry has to accept hounds on their

front sidewalk patio! Baby Boomers remember the lovable cartoon character that ran in the early 1960s, and was syndicated throughout their childhood. Well, this café has nothing to do with that. In fact, the young, hip clientele probably never heard of Huckleberry Hound. Instead, the patrons equate this clean, contemporary hot-spot with homemade granola, fennel sausage links, kale and pine nut salad, and decadent sweets. The vibe is casually cool with high-quality food. Arnold, the "Governator" and his wife, Maria, eat here. Take-out is an option if dinner is desired after the closing time of 7 p.m. on weekdays and 5 p.m. on weekends.

KREATION KAFÉ
1023 Montana Avenue - B, Santa Monica, CA 90403
(310) 458-4880 • No website ($$)
....

Kreation Kafé takes healthy to the nth degree. No freezers or microwaves are used. As part of the Santa Monica Certified Green Business initiative, they offer local farmer's organic produce when possible. Protein-rich quinoa grain and Omega-3 fatty acid flax meal are kitchen staples. Breakfast pancakes have California pistachios and Acai syrup drizzled on top. Lunch salads and sandwiches

with free-range chicken and Niman Ranch ground beef satisfy carnivores. "Kreative" dinner tapas combine iron-fortified rice with a vegetable and caramelized mushroom saute. Pooches dine at the front sidewalk tables. It's open from 8 a.m. to 10 p.m. daily. The to-go menu is also environmentally conscious; it's printed on recycled paper with soy ink.

BLUE PLATE
1415 Montana Avenue, Santa Monica, CA 90403
(310) 260-8877 • www.blueplatesantamonica.com ($$)
....

The neighborhood eatery resides in a quiet pocket of Santa Monica, a few blocks east of frenetic Ocean Avenue. It's known to locals as their "kitchen away from home." Chef Violet Robles balances hearty and healthy meals. Two tables in front of the corner restaurant host Fifi and family. Breakfast includes stacks, sides, and other stuff, while lunch supplies soups, salads, and sandwiches. Artisan brewskis and boutique winery varietals energize patrons' dinner conversations. Care packages with home-cooked meals evoke a small-town feel. What better way to say "Congratula-tions," "Feel Better," or to have a picnic in the park, than a quart of Chicken Rice Gumbo and roasted turkey on fresh baked bread with cookies for dessert?

LA GRANDE ORANGE
2000 Main Street, Santa Monica, CA 90405
(310) 396-9145 • www.lagrandeorangesm.com ($$)

Breakfast starts at 6:30 a.m. and dinner ends at 11 p.m.; that's a lot of freshly prepared meals being cranked out at the Ocean Park joint. Customers order at the counter, get a number, and a server delivers the food to the table. American classics are the specialties – an organic Turkey Meatloaf Sandwich with Mushroom Gravy, a Grilled Asparagus Caesar Salad, and Dixie Pan-Fried Chicken. K9s must dine on the patio and cannot be left unattended. That's an interesting feat if dining alone, but adjacent patrons usually keep an eye on your pooch while you order inside. Totally unrelated… their website is so Santa Monica, or SaMo, as the locals call it.

ROSTI TUSCAN KITCHEN
931 Montana Avenue, Santa Monica, CA 90403
(310) 393-3236 • www.rostituscankitchen.com ($$)

Three locations, Santa Monica, Beverly Hills, and Encino, attest to the Italian eatery's popularity. For over 18 years, its been serving lunch and dinner, seven days a week. The family restaurant is instrumental in its neighborhood, participating in fundraisers and providing *bambinis* with a free children's meal if they read over 10 hours at the Santa Monica Public Library. Two and four-leggers drool over the Pasta Fagioli White Bean and Potato Soup, Eggplant Parm Pizza Pie, and salads doused in made-from-scratch cucumber mint dressing. To-go picnic boxes with a choice of salads, pasta, sandwiches, and fresh baked cookies are also available. That's amore!

Play

THE SOUTH BAY BICYCLE TRAIL
(A portion is the Santa Monica Beach Bike Path)
Between Pacific Palisades and Torrance
(800) 544-5319 (Santa Monica Convention & Visitors Bureau)
(310) 319-6263 • www.santamonica.com
....

The 22-mile ribbon of concrete is the longest beach path of its kind in the world. About two-and-a-half of those miles border the ocean along Santa Monica beach. It's the quintessential Southern California experience, with tanned skateboarders and mountain bikes darting among walkers. On weekends the pedestrian traffic is a bit like the 405 freeway at rush hour. Cycles can be rented at numerous locations along the trail. Lapdogs are better off riding in the basket.

SANTA MONICA PIER
Intersection of Ocean Avenue and Colorado Avenue
Santa Monica, CA 90401
(310) 458-8900 • www.santamonicapier.org
....

On September 9, 2009 the city of Santa Monica celebrated the centennial of Southern California's most documented pier. For 70 of those years, its iconic neon sign at the portal has been recognizable to visitors worldwide.

Car buffs identify the icon as the western terminus of Route 66. The 1,600-foot-long amusement quay draws over four million visitors annually, and is open 24 hours a day, 365 days a year. Admission is complimentary for pooches and people. Pacific Park, the ride and game area, is a Fido-free zone. There is plenty of plank to walk, as well as street performers and artists' masterpieces to gawk at. Souvenir shops sell pier memorabilia, shells, and beads. Munchies abound.

PALISADES PARK

Ocean Avenue, between Colorado Avenue and San Vicente Boulevard
Santa Monica, CA 90401
(800) 544-5319 (Santa Monica Convention & Visitors Bureau)
(310) 319-6263 • www.santamonica.com

....

The 26-acre pooch playground sits atop red sandstone bluffs overlooking the Santa Monica beach. It boasts a 1.6-mile walking path,

busy with roller bladers and joggers. Countless palm trees cast a reprieve from the sun for exercising pooches. The rose garden's pergola has vines sprawled among its cross beams, and public art sculptures are intermittent. A Visitors Information kiosk provides maps, souvenir tee-shirts and knowledgeable travel counselors.

Fetch

MONTANA AVENUE

Between 7th Street and 17th Street, Santa Monica, CA 90403
www.santamonica.com • www.wagwagwag.com
www.leonaedmiston.com • www.jonathanadler.com
....

Boutiques and bistros residing along the ten-block enclave are both hip and humble. The tree-lined street in a residential neighborhood near swanky Brentwood is Santa Monica's most pet-friendly area. Most of the 150 businesses are privately owned. Four chirping parakeets and two senior dogs accompany the proprietor of Cabana Clothing to work every day. Ardent fans of The Wagging Tail rave about the b.b. simon dog collars. Australian designer

Leona Edmiston has one of her two U.S.A. stores here showcasing the simple, timeless Jersey dresses she's known for. Jonathan Adler's kitschy menagerie of wares include hand-loomed wool dog beds with matching sofa pillows, and custom whimsical pooch paintings.

BRENTWOOD COUNTRY MART

San Vicente Boulevard and 26th Street, Santa Monica, CA 90402
(310) 451-9877
www.brentwoodcountrymart.com • www.calypso-celle.com
www.apartmentnumber9.com • www.turpanonline.com
....

Located in one of the wealthiest neighborhoods in L.A., the Mart is a bit of old Americana among affluent Westside homes. A recent facelift of the original 1948 red barn with white trim resulted in an identical, yet more youthful façade with the charm of yore. Inside,

27 high-end boutiques share space with a barber, cobbler, and general store. Home furnishings and casual women's styles can be found at Calypso. Men's runway fashions fill Apartment Number 9. Turpan lifestyle store is a mish-mash of housewares, clothing, and toys. Marie Mason Apothecary is a family run shop, often with husband, wife, and tween daughter working. The alfresco food court is home to the legendary Reddi Chick rotisserie chicken eatery, said to be the best in the county. You and the pooch can be the judge of that. On Sundays from 9 a.m. till 2 p.m., pony rides and a petting zoo entertain children.

THIRD STREET PROMENADE
Between Broadway and Wilshire Boulevard, Santa Monica, CA 90401
www.downtownsm.com

Over 200 chain stores, independent shops, and restaurants constitute the outdoor pedestrian promenade. Pottery Barn, Banana Republic, and equally well-liked retailers lure a steady stream of tourists and locals. A huge fountain with decorative animal topiar-

ies anchors one end of the three-block mall. Street musicians perform for onlookers hoping to have a few greenbacks tossed their way. Those in need of a pick-me-up grab a cuppa java at Caffé Bellagio with the pooch. The lunch crowd refuels with to-go meals, enjoyed on one of the benches shaded by Jacaranda trees. Wednesdays and Saturdays the Santa Monica Farmers Market sets up along the west side of the esplanade. Celebrity chefs frequent the weekday market to cull the quality fruits, breads, and vegetables served in their famous eateries. No wonder Zagat declared SaMo to be the "best neighborhood for dining" in all of Southern California.

MALIBU LUMBER YARD
3835 Cross Creek Road, Malibu, CA 90265
MALIBU COUNTRY MART
3939 Cross Creek Road, Malibu, CA 90265
(310) 456-7395 • www.malibucountrymart.com
www.jamesperse.com • www.crumbs.com • www.aliceandolivia.com
....

With 75 miles of coastline in L.A., why not take a scenic drive up
the PCH to Malibu's open-air shopping plazas about a dozen miles
north of Santa Monica. The Lumber Yard is the newest addition
to the celebrity enclaves retail scene. The grand opening drew
Matthew McCon-

aughey and singer
Jewel. Exclusive
boutiques and
cafes surround a
hardwood deck
ornamented with
two eleven-foot tall
fish tanks, and teak
furniture. A ping-
pong table outside
James Perse
apparel stokes
shoppers' competi-
tive fires between purchases. Sanctuary Clothing is a "pop-up"
store that stays in its space only a few months before traveling
to another city. Crumbs cupcakes are worth every calorie, as is
Dylan's chocolate bars at Alice + Olivia. Adjacent Malibu Country
Mart adds 65 more places to spend your dough. Its six acres, with
a large playground and grassy quad, summon kiddies and the family pooch to enjoy the sunshine.

HEALTHY SPOT
8525 Santa Monica Boulevard, Santa Monica, CA 90401
1110 Wilshire Boulevard, West Hollywood, CA 90069
(310) 458-2004 • (310) 657-2400 • www.healthyspotla.com
....

This daycare and spa is a healthy spot for your healthy Spot. It
offers quality products and services. You can't get more cutting-

edge than blueberry and plum pet facials, milk and honey baths, and moisturizing paw rubs. Anxious dogs may require the heal-

ing hands of the Reiki therapist – 30 or 60 minute sessions are available. Organic and vegetarian canine cuisine fills shelves and refrigerators, alongside homeopathic oral meds, FouFou brand toys, and K9 art. Spayed or neutered pups, 30 pounds or less, with proof of current vaccination records are welcome to spend the day at the inside grassy play area, complete with a red fire hydrant.

Veterinarian

ASEC
Animal Surgical & Emergency Center
1535 South Sepulveda Boulevard, Los Angeles, CA 90025
24 Hour Emergency (310) 473-1561
Surgery Department (310) 473-5906
www.ASECvets.com

....

Stay

THE CRESCENT
403 North Crescent Drive, Beverly Hills, CA 90210 🐕🐕🐕🐕
(310) 247-0505 • www.crescentbh.com ($$)
....

The 1930s villa is hidden behind mature trees on one of Beverly Hills' main thoroughfares in the Golden Triangle. Once used to house silent movie stars, it's now a premiere inn, steps from famous Rodeo Drive. The stars still hang out here, but they're not silent. Movie contracts between moguls are bartered on the front patio over drinks. They come here because of the personalized service and privacy. The 34-year-old owner sets a hip ambiance, with a minimalist, uncluttered scene.

Pups have access to the majority of this 35 room *pied-a-terre*. Sleeping quarters are petit and unpretentious with bare walls, dark furniture, and poured concrete bathrooms. Platform beds are low enough for furry friends of all sizes to effortlessly leap onto. Customized iPods in every room, loaded with a jazz and reggae play list, lull them to the land of zzz's. The pet fee is $50, which entitles

Bowser to Ikea *Bastis Krona* food bowls and a *Rajtan* jar full of treats. In-room massages – for people – are offered in lieu of a pool on property.

Boe restaurant serves brunch and dinner alfresco. The name is an acronym for the Greek and Roman idols Bacchus, Orpheus, and Epicurius. Eight cozy tables share a polished cement patio with modular sofas and Beverly Hills' only indoor-outdoor fireplace. Aromatic Shrimp Cassoulet and Chicken Paillard contend for favorite meal. The bartender's Basil Gimlet and Ginger Mai Tai are drink winners. Informal sake, beer, and wine tastings are offered periodically. Morning coffee and afternoon tea are equally enjoyable according to a local gentleman who visits the eatery weekly with his German Shepherd.

THE PENINSULA BEVERLY HILLS
9882 South Santa Monica Boulevard, Beverly Hills, CA 90212
(310) 551-2888 • www.peninsula.com ($$$$)

This is pure Five Diamond elegance from the minute you cross the threshold of the 196 room estate on a quiet block of Beverly Hills. The flagship Hong Kong property was built on a peninsula in 1928, hence the trademark name. With only nine hotels worldwide, Peninsula has perfected tailored service for each patron, including pooches.

There are usually two Rovers in residence most days. Management realizes guests treat their dogs as family members, so The Peninsula does, too. Perhaps a reason 65% of customers are repeat visitors. Size is of no concern, but impeccable manners are of utmost importance, and a $35 fee is charged daily. The enviable lifestyle includes an in-room Pampered Puppy menu serving beef burgers, strip steak, or a "Tail Shakin' not Stirred Martini," sans hooch, it's only beef bouillon. An Ultrasuede dog bed and a fluffy towel monogrammed with the pooch's name depict the rarefied standards set by the hotel, as do the parent's personalized Frette pillowcases. Inoffensive beiges and browns decorate the room. The neutral setting is conducive for guests who bring their own furniture when staying for months, even years. The bathroom marble is quarried specifically for the upscale chain, and Italian Davi toiletries produced by Carlo Mondovi − grandson of wine-maker Robert Mondovi − are exclusive to the hotel group.

Hollywood heavyweights frequent Belvedere restaurant. The one pet-friendly corner table on the patio provides perfect seating for "star" gazing, so to speak. The Living Room serves afternoon tea daily, to the accompaniment of a classical harpist. Arrange for a pet-sitter with Les Clefs d'Ore concierge, James Little, touted as "The Best Concierge in the World" by GQ Europe. Famed Peninsula Pages, dressed in crisp white uniforms and matching pillbox hats, gladly walk Fido for a $10 fee, which they keep, not the hotel. They've been known to snap a photo of your lovable licker and frame the picture in silver as a souvenir for guests.

The Peninsula Academy will arrange for guests to star in their own movie. A producer and camera crew spend the day filming mutts and masters surfing, sightseeing, or whatever they desire. The footage is edited into a DVD to take home. Those who want to "sound like a star" can work with dialect coach, Bob Corff, who taught Cate Blanchett to speak like Katharine Hepburn in "The Aviator."

THE BEVERLY HILLS HOTEL AND BUNGALOWS
9641 Sunset Boulevard, Beverly Hills, CA 90210
(310) 276-2251 • www.beverlyhillshotel.com ($$$$)

Perched majestically above Sunset Boulevard, L.A.'s "Pink Palace" still reigns supreme over her countless successors. Opened in 1912, she was the first major structure in the area and named after the builder's hometown of Beverly Farms, Massachusetts. In the early 1990s, after various owners, including petroleum moguls and celebrities, the Sultan of Brunei purchased the hotel for a reputed

$110 million, and spent millions more restoring her to today's eminence, where Fido the pooch is now addressed as "Phideaux."

The trademark pink and green color palette is tastefully laced throughout the property, starting with the Porte-Cochere's jade-and-white striped awning. Signature banana leaf wallpaper lines hallways, cotton-candy hued uniforms adorn the housekeeping staff, and bar stools at the Fountain Coffee Shop have the familiar blush tint.

Carpeted outdoor pathways canopied by towering bird-of-paradise lead to the 21 bungalows where Phideaux is permitted to slumber. The casitas are glamorous bubbles of Grecian marble, gold bathroom fixtures, and fabric-covered walls, complete with in-room mani/pedis and baths drawn by the butler.

Intrinsically aware of the bond between people and pets, the "Canine Connoisseur Program" outfits each cabana with a custom-designed dog bed and ceramic bowls. The $200 pet fee provides dog walkers 24/7, and if requested at check-in, personalized treats will be delivered. Should the pooch have "luggage," a bellman willingly unpacks the belongings.

Two pet dining options are in the main hotel. The Fountain Coffee Shop, serving breakfast, lunch, and light dinner since 1949, accedes to Phideaux being tethered within eyesight just beyond the glass doorway. The Citrus Garden is the second alternative. Meals are delivered via room service to the few tables on the patio.

With a 25 pound weight limit, the 12-acres of lush landscaping more often than not, provide pups with enough exercise. Less lack-adaisical lapdogs can run free at the Will Rogers Memorial Park across the street. It's an ideal setting for a pet-sitter to take dogs, should guests want to test the spas' "Diamond Perfection" body microdermabrasion with real diamonds and pearls, or the "Caviar Firming Facial" featuring sturgeon roe.

RAFFLES L'ERMITAGE BEVERLY HILLS
9291 Burton Way, Beverly Hills, CA 90210
(310) 278-3344 • www.lermitagebh.com ($$$$)

Irrefutably, Beverly Hills is one of L.A.'s classiest neighborhoods, and Raffles L'Ermitage follows suite. Its unobtrusive façade blends into the landscaping, making it appear to be a home on the residential block. The discreet decor is infused with an Asian tranquility of silk and soft leather furnishings. A 24 hour flexible room check-in/check-out policy allows guests to arrive and depart at will. Business cards and hotel stationary imprinted with clients' names and in-residence phone numbers are presented along with room keys.

The Pool Terrace and Amrita Spa are on the rooftop, have 360-degree views of the city. Have the concierge call a pet-sitter and check out this retreat. Clean, simple architecture creates an unencumbered feel. Yellow orchids float among river rocks in the spa fountain. Tunes play in the background, as weary muscles are massaged into submission.

Both of the hotel's dining choices don't permit pooches. JAAN signature eatery has superlative dishes of Roasted Chestnut Soup and Vanilla Sea Scallops. The Writer's Bar is a comfy spot serving snacks and cocktails. While pets are excluded, they are certainly not ignored. Rover's room-service menu surpasses most fast-food chow. Grilled filet of beef with organic rice and brown gravy is premium, as is the chicken consomme for those trying to stay under the obligatory 35 pound weight restriction. A chauffeured limo transports pups and people to an afternoon shopping spree at Rodeo Drive four blocks away, or a romp in Beverly Gardens Park. These excursions, along with a dog bed and bowls, are included in the $150 pet fee.

Before retiring in the evening, read a few pages from a tiny book of "Stories For Bedtime" provided in the room. Nighty night.

SLS HOTEL

465 South La Cienega Boulevard, Los Angeles, CA 90048
(310) 247-0400 • www.slshotels.com ($$$)

....

Hotels don't get much cooler than SLS. Awe is ones first reaction. Its Four Diamond rating seems too rudimentary; four crowns is more fitting. French designer Philippe Starck's imaginative deviation from the decorating norm makes this place tremendously distinct. A Hollywood-style red carpet leads to the lobby. Lighted

Lucite deer heads hang above mosaic planters large enough to live in, and love seats are made of antlers. White sofas sit beside shelves lined with books dedicated to L.A.'s two loves – fashion and music. Smoky mirrors cover much of the wall space.

The initials SLS are not an abbreviation, but a springboard for sayings printed throughout the hotel – Soft Like Silk (bathrobe label), Scorched Lips Satiated (water bottle), So Long, Sweetie (the bill), and Seek Light Sustenance (paper napkins). The 297 rooms have only graced the cacophonous city since December, 2008 and SLS has welcomed pooches 40 pounds or less since day one with a $120 pet fee.

Starck conceived his guest rooms unlike others. The bathroom and sleeping quarters are separated by a wall on rollers, so one can have privacy, or not. Austrian crystal glassware is beside the sink. A 40" plasma television screen is hidden inside a mirror, making it invisible when not in use. Cherry cotton candy and honey wheat pretzels in the snack tray let guests decide whether to be a sinner or saint. A shadow box on the wall contains seven items, each accom-

panied by a few words. "Be bad" tempts above a piece of choco-late, "feel better" urge the bath salts, "be good" rests above a fresh apple, a postcard coaxes to "share," et al. Massages from Ciel Spa are deliverable for an extra charge. No detail is unattended, includ-ing origami pet food bowls and a faux fur dog bed.

The tongue-in-cheek room directory briefs visitors on Beverly Hills protocol: " an Air Kiss is for individuals who don't want to get up-close-and-personal, accompanied with a faint whisper of 'mwah' several inches from the cheek." Dog walkers charge " a $20 fee to leave the property and access to the finest fire hydrants in L.A.."

The front portico is a hot place for sipping tipples and congregating with traveling hounds, as this is the only area where they are permitted. Room service or a pup-sitter are the dining options. Should the latter be chosen, check out The Bazaar, where three eateries in a yawning space are demarcated by different color palettes. Bar Centro has a raw bar, Rojo Y Blanca serves tapas, The Patisserie, sweets, and Moss is a roving retail emporium. Unique.

AVALON HOTEL
9400 West Olympic Boulevard, Beverly Hills, CA 90212
(866) 270-9051 • (310) 277-5221 • www.avalonbeverlyhills.com ($$$)
....

Avalon is more of a motel than a hotel. Three low-rise buildings named Beverly, Canon, and Olympic make up 86 retro rooms. Olympic's courtyard is the hub of activity with an hourglass shaped pool, private outdoor dining cabanas, and the signature Oliverio restaurant. The Mid-Century architecture, with guest room balconies overlooking the terrace below, grant a birds-eye view of "Hollywoodites" lunching on the chef's Italian cuisine, or vacationers test-driving the California way of life. L.A.'s younger crowd is lured here by designer Kelly Wearstler's less highfalutin version of luxury. The entryway's vintage furniture boasts a rare 1967 Italian Archizoom modular sofa. A geometric ceiling mural enhances the Doris Day, Rock Hudson-era motif.

Those traveling with pets stay in the more pedestrian Canon building across the street. Fifteen rooms with well-worn, improvised furniture seem disconnected from the festivities over yonder. The rationale for canines staying in Canon are its accompanying patios, although their miniscule size is inadequate even for the 25 pounds or less weight restriction imposed by the manager. A $100 fee per stay is issued and there are no pet beds, bowls, or sitters available. Dining options are a toaster oven/microwave combo stacked on the kitchenette countertop or 24 hour room service.

The Olympic building lobby is pet-friendly and a great place to meet people. One need only relax there momentarily with their pup to realize passing patrons find it irresistible to stop for a pooch smooch. Conversations ensue, and

before long fast friends are made while sipping Antioxidant POM Wonderful cocktails together. The eclectic clientele of videographers, PR execs, and other industry wannabes weave fascinating tales.

Kibble

THE FARM OF BEVERLY HILLS
439 North Beverly Drive, Beverly Hills, CA 90210
(310) 273-5578 • www.thefarmofbeverlyhills.com ($$$$)
....

It's not a farm, it's an all-day casual café claiming to cook food like Mom would make…perhaps, if Mom were Nigella Lawson. The Beverly Hills spot – one of three L.A. locations – hums with action in the heart of the Golden Triangle. To-go pastries offer a quick breakfast. "Farmeooh" cookies – large, soft homemade versions of Oreos – provide hours of sugar buzz. Try the warm pear and brie sandwich on toasted raisin walnut bread. The front patio appeals to diners who wouldn't think of leaving their coddled critters at the hotel. Filet Mignon, Turkey Lasagna, Short Ribs, Pan Roasted Tilapia… they're all like Mom used to make.

M CAFÉ

9433 Brighton Way, Beverly Hills, CA 90210
(310) 858-8459 • www.mcafedechaya.com ($$)
....

The European café serves contemporary macrobiotic cuisine, which dates back to Hippocrates, who used the word to describe

healthy people. Grains, veggies, beans, seafood, and no processed foods are the premise for the nutritious cooking. Not a scintilla of taste is sacrificed when preparing meals. The Scrambled Tofu Breakfast with Sweet Potato Hash Browns…yummy. California Clubs with tempeh "bacon," and a large selection of salads are savored outdoors under yellow canvas umbrellas. Tart lemonade combines agave, salt, and H2O. Menus change seasonally, but pups' love for the delicious fare doesn't

COUPA CAFÉ

419 North Canon Drive, Beverly Hills, CA 90210
(310) 385-0420 • www.coupacafe.com ($$)
....

Denizens from Venezuela replicate such feasts as *polvorosa de pollo* — shredded chicken, sweet peppers, tomatoes, olives, and sugar cane pulp in a flaky pie crust. The *especialidades* of the house are white cornmeal griddle cakes, or arepas, stuffed with anything from shark to cheese to chicken salad. The patio buzzes with lively prattle fueled by South American wines and dark, rich coffee imported from the home country. The wait staff supply water bowls for *perros*, who rest under the leaves of potted banana trees. From early morning pastries to late night *empanadas*, this Latino gastrohub sizzles.

208 RODEO BEVERLY HILLS
208 Via Rodeo Drive, Beverly Hills, CA 90210
(310) 275-2428 • www.208rodeo.com ($$$$)
....

Interminably chic people dine at this bistro located at the hottest intersection in L.A., Wilshire Boulevard and Rodeo Drive; namely, Two Rodeo, where the Versace boutique displays haute couture and Tiffany's baubles shimmer for miles. An Italianate cobblestone road leads to the restaurant poised directly across the street from the Beverly Wilshire Hotel, where *Pretty Woman* was filmed. The cuisine has extra panache; the goat cheese salad

is topped with shiitake mushrooms, and ravioli is transformed with spring peas. The 208 Parfait's infusion of fresh berries, low-fat yogurt, and granola is a breakfast bestseller. People-watching is phenomenal, even the four-legged kind.

XI'AN
362 North Canon Drive, Beverly Hills, CA 90210
(310) 275-3345 • www.xian90210.com ($$)
....

Xi'an is named for the ancient capitol of China, whose present day claim to fame is the Terra Cotta Warriors – an army of clay soldiers buried with the First Emperor. The primordial city's location at one end of the 5,000 mile Silk Road provided access to spices and other wares being traded on the route. These culinary tastes are the genesis for the eatery's four page menu. Enjoy the Claypot

Chicken swathed in ginger, basil and sizzling onions, and Whole Cod marinated in a pungent sauce. Pups can sneak a smidgen of rice under the patio table.

MADAME CHOCOLAT BEVERLY HILLS

212 North Canon Drive, Beverly Hills, CA 90210
(310) 247-9990 • www.madame-chocolat.com ($)

....

Only one morsel is needed to confirm that chocolatier Hasty Torres is supreme at her craft. The boutique's velvety bon bons with classic Jonnie Walker Blue Label whiskey in dark chocolate ganache are eye-rolling luscious. Milk-chocolate-coated Cheerios add a new twist to a child's snack. A sprinkling of tables sit on the front sidewalk, inviting patrons to delight in a cup of hot chocolate, while gawking at the numerous Maseratis purring down the busy street. Imbibe alone, as chocolate is poisonous to dogs.

Play

TOUR DU JOUR

9663 Santa Monica Boulevard; Ste. 680, Beverly Hills, CA 90210
(310) 659-2929 • www.tourdujour.net ($$$$)

....

This private tour company is ranked in the top 1% of travel ambassadors in the Americas. Tours run two hours, a half-day or a full-day, with custom jaunts available. Hotel pick-up and drop-off is included. Lap size pooches can ride along. Jaguars and Cadillac Escalades are chauffeured by local guides with a flair for witty repartee. The Heart of the City trip views exteriors of Walt Disney Concert Hall, Cathedral of Our Lady of the Angels, et al. You can stand in movie stars' footprints at Grauman's Chinese Theater and check out celebrity estates on the L.A. Short Story excursion. For those who want scandal, the Hollywood Chills tour visits murder, suicide and overdose locations.

WALKING IN THE FOOTSTEPS OF CELEBRITIES
239 South Beverly Drive, Beverly Hills, CA 90212
(800) 345-2210 (Beverly Hills Conference & Visitors Bureau)
(310) 248-1015 • www.lovebeverlyhills.com
....

Ever want to walk a mile in celebritie's shoes? Now's your chance. The circuitous 2.5-mile self-guided tour meanders throughout the Golden Triangle past Gucci and Prada mega stores, The Shave of Beverly Hills grooming hot spot, and The Paley Center for Media,

which archives over 140,000 radio and television programs. Rest the paws and dine like a movie star at The Blvd., Beverly Wilshire Hotel's alfresco eatery. A few blocks north, Sprinkles Cupcakes panders to patrons wanting to indulge in red velvet confectionaries.

Download a map from the "Love Beverly Hills" website.

MULHOLLAND SCENIC DRIVE

7036 Mulholland Drive (Hollywood Bowl Overlook) to
31100 Mulholland Drive (Seminole Overlook), Los Angeles, CA
(310) 589-3200 (Santa Monica Mountain Conservancy)
www.LAMountains.com (Map)

....

The breathtaking drive starts west of the 101 freeway in Hollywood, and twists fifty-five miles through the Santa Monica Mountains. Twenty-four of the miles are in the City of Los Angeles, with
the remainder extending to Calabasas. It was constructed in 1924
to transport residents to the beaches. Today, dream homes owned
by cinema A-listers such as Jack Nicholson and Warren Beatty are
perched precariously on the hillsides. Numerous overlooks, maintained by a local conservation group, invite motorists to absorb the
city and ocean views below.

BEVERLY GARDENS PARK

North Santa Monica Boulevard, between Wilshire Boulevard and
Doheny Boulevard, Beverly Hills, CA 90210
(310) 285-2536 (Beverly Hills City Hall) • www.beverlyhills.org

....

Beverly Gardens is a two-mile, narrow "green belt" which runs

alongside Santa Monica Boulevard,
separating multi-million-dollar homes
from the shopping/hotel district. A
granite jogging trail spans its length, with
ample shade trees for pooches to cool
off. Whimsical stainless steel sculptures
painted in bright Matisse hues dot the
manicured lawn. A statue dubbed "Hunt-
er and Hounds" depicts a young man and
two Bloodhounds. An impressive cactus
collection extends one city block. Farther
west, the Electric Fountain has been a
mainstay for almost 80 years.

RODEO DRIVE, TWO RODEO

Between South Santa Monica Boulevard and Wilshire Boulevard
Beverly Hills, CA 90210
(310) 248-1015 (Beverly Hills Conference & Visitors Bureau)
www.lovebeverlyhills.com • www.tworodeo.com
....

Rodeo is the shoppertainment capital of the world, boasting a
veritable "Who's Who" of the fashion industry. Retail heavyweights
call Rodeo Drive home; Prada, Fendi, Bottega Veneta, Chanel,
and Valentino all
have boutiques

along this street
of dreams. The
private-jet set shops
here. A few retail-
ers relegate pups to
window-shopping
only, but the major-
ity greet them with
a big grin. Two
Rodeo's cove of
25 exclusive stores
and eateries is
nirvana, with Tiffany & Co., Versace, and Jimmy Choo as tenants.
One block north is Rodeo's unpretentious stepsister, Beverly Drive,
where Banana Republic, Crate and Barrel, The Gap, and more sell
their wares.

TASCHEN

354 North Beverly Drive, Beverly Hills, CA 90210
(310) 274-4300 • www.taschen.com
....

Extraordinary coffee table books from the simple to the sublime are
sold in this cool store. The narrow, open space of dark mahogany
displays gobs of obscure editions with stellar pictures. Leather sofas
for perusing pages and conference-size tables to ruminate about
eye-catching spreads encourage extended visits. Classical art, pop

culture, travel, and film icons are a few genres represented. Many VIP's desire to be the muse for one of Taschen's photographic masterpieces. Designer Valentino himself signed his 576-page homage while onlookers sipped champagne. Limited publications with his actual sketches fetched $1,500, while the masses purchased the reproduced $70 version. Fido fans covet A Thousand Dogs in paperback, chronicling the esteemed pooch.

DOGGIE STYLES

9467 Charleville Boulevard, Beverly Hills, CA 90210
(310) 278-0031 • www.doggiestylesonline.com

....

Beverly Hills glitterati isn't limited to just people; haute dogs don Swarovski crystals and Juicy Couture, too. "Premium Products for the Pampered Pooch" is owner Michael Campbell's motto. His dream team – Buttons the French Bulldog and Boxer, Hemi – aid customers in deciding between Cece Kent Taos or Emre NY Paco carriers, and test-lie on Dutchie beds for comfort. WoWo's line of wall-mounted food bowls are both sleek and practical. Periodic gatherings mingle party animals and merrymakers for a bit of bubbly and patisserie puppy treats.

Veterinarian

ASEC

Animal Surgical & Emergency Center
1535 South Sepulveda Boulevard, Los Angeles, CA 90025
24 Hour Emergency (310) 473-1561
Surgery Department (310) 473-5906
www.ASECvets.com

....

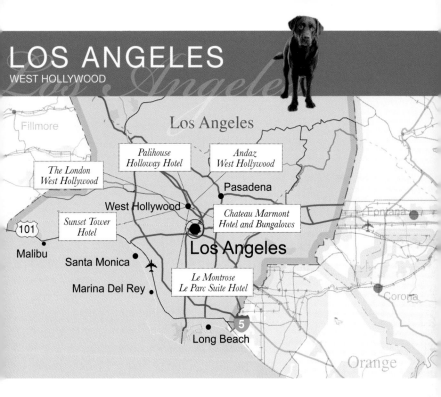

LOS ANGELES
WEST HOLLYWOOD

Stay

SUNSET TOWER HOTEL
8358 Sunset Boulevard, Hollywood, CA 90069 🐕🐕🐕🐕
(323) 654-7100 • www.sunsettowerhotel.com ($$$$)
....

When a hotel has a Director of Goodwill and Canine Relations, it's obvious the owner is gaga for dogs. The owner's Beagle, Bisou, holds the prestigious position, which is substantial at the 1920s fifteen-story, Art Deco landmark.

It was once a luxury apartment building where Joan Crawford, and Frank Sinatra lived, and John Wayne kept his pet cow on the patio for fresh milk. Later years saw it fall into disrepair until an 18-month restoration returned the tower to its "Golden Era" class. Preserved is the façade's ornamentation and the interior walnut paneling with brass inlay, along side 21st century upgrades. The

Sunset has a different agenda than its more modern neighbors. The latest starlet is not revered here; sophistication is preferred.

Benevolent Bisou provides in-room dog beds made of taupe suede with The Sunset Tower embroidered in cream thread, and a bone-shaped dog bowl with the same insignia. A welcome letter familiarizes guests with the William S. Hart off-leash park directly beside the hotel, and nearby day care, doggie boutiques, and pet-friendly restaurants.

Bugsy Siegel's apartment, until he was evicted for running an illegal gambling ring, is now the Tower Bar. The cozy 80-seat restaurant is evocative of more formal days, with waiters dressed in white jackets, addressing diners as "Sir" and "Ma'me." A framed letter from former resident Truman Capote hangs on the wall. The gracious hospitality is extended to pups at the peripheral lounge tables.

The Terrace eatery offers an informal setting overlooking the pool, and great views of the city. Pups and people can grab breakfast, lunch, and dinner here. Bisou has arranged for his fellow four-legged friends to have their own menu, which can also be served poolside.

CHATEAU MARMONT HOTEL AND BUNGALOWS
8221 Sunset Boulevard, Hollywood, CA 90046
(323) 656-1010 • www.chateaumarmont.com ($$$$)

Secluded by a foliage fortress in the Hollywood Hills above Tinseltown, the iconic 1929 grand dame looms majestic above the frenetic action on Sunset Boulevard. Not only does this celebrity hideaway cater to Hollywood hot shots, it rolls out the red carpet for pooches, as well. Wherever human guests are permitted, furry friends may follow. The inclusiveness is an extension of the accommodating mentality this hotel has perfected.

Contrary to the nouveau, ultra sleek hotels in the area, the Marmont has maintained her classic early 20th century décor. Velveteen armchairs, tasseled drapes, oriental carpets, and dark hardwood floors culminate in an homage to a bygone era when the likes of Greta Garbo frequented the French-inspired estate.

In the course of a day, the Chateau will host at least a handful of media magnates, whether it's Cameron Diaz dining with friends on the patio, Saturday Night Live comedian Chris Kattan enjoying time with his wife, or Richard Lewis relaxing with a good read in the lounge. Nobody fawns over them; all the guests are treated equally.

The sun patio with its cushioned chaises and heated pool summons paws and pieds to sit a spell. Families with children spend hours splashing away the afternoon. Lush groves of fragrant flowers and dense trees muffle the giggles from the neighboring cottages. Standard rooms in the main building are generous, with high ceilings and period furniture, which pets are duly charged $150 to share with their owner. A brown paper bag of treats identified with your  pooch's name and two food bowls with a can opener, should Fido eat wet food, are en suite.

Evening hours will see the lounge and garden terrace buzzing with industry executives discussing contracts, mutual-fund brokers extolling their profits, and merrymakers celebrating special occasions. As the hours pass, the chatter rises a few decibels. Partying goes late into the night. No photos are permitted; it's a movie star safe haven. Servers flutter throughout the crowd, catering to idiosyncrasies. This is what Marmont does best; the old girl still has it.

PALIHOUSE HOLLOWAY HOTEL

8465 Holloway Drive, West Hollywood, CA 90069 🐕🐕🐕🐕

(323) 656-4100 • www.palihouse.com ($$$)

....

Palihouse is more European casual than L.A. showy. The lobby and public areas are one floor below street level, utilizing every inch they can, while also abiding by WeHo's five-floor ordinance on new construction. The receptionists are called House Masters, and are on duty from 7a.m. until 11p.m.. A spacious den off the entryway, with well-used sofas and perpetual music from the stereo is the gathering spot for those with two or four gams. Vacationers and

Angelenos' hang out there. "Hudson," an aging Golden Retriever, comes daily with his pop, who snags the free WiFi. No one minds. It's a come one, come all pet policy with a 125 pound weight limit. The ambiguous $185 pooch fee for overnight hounds is case-specific, determined by the duration of the stay.

Guest rooms overlook the outdoor courtyard brasserie. They are tastefully designed with chocolate carpets, pin-stripped walls, and huge framed art leaning against exposed brick walls. The closet holds a washer/dryer combo. A voyeuristic window in the shower peeks into the sitting area, and visa versa. The old wive's tale about a dog's tongue being cleaner than a human's comes in handy when the dishes in the room's kitchenette double as Bowser's bowl at mealtime. To reduce the carbon footprint, housekeeping cleans once every three days; there's an extra charge if daily upkeep is desired.

Daily nourishment falls on the shoulders of the patio restaurant. Croissants, coffee, and award-worthy chocolate chip cookies start the day off early, while Steak Frites and Lamb Burgers are paraded from the kitchen well after dark. The Astroturf-clad rooftop hosts Happy Hour Wednesday through Sunday, as well as a mixer once a month for the GLBT community.

ANDAZ WEST HOLLYWOOD

8401 West Sunset Boulevard, West Hollywood, CA 90069
(323) 656-1234 • www.westhollywood.andaz.com ($$)
....

Smack dab in the heart of Sunset Strip is the area's newest hotel - Andaz - which means "personal style" in Hindu. It neighbors the House of Blues, The Comedy Store, and multi-million-dollar Hollywood homes. Vacationers may recognize the hot spot from its 1960s "Riot Hyatt" days, when Jim Morrison hung from the balcony by his fingertips, Keith Richards mooned onlookers, and rock legends partied hardy. Only the structure remains from those wild days; the persona and interior have been revamped.

Gone is the traditional reception desk. Instead, "hosts" dressed in street clothing greet guests at the valet out front. Their friendly demeanor replaces a uniform and name tag. They usher travelers to the lounge's cushy sofas and offer a glass of complimentary wine. A hand-held credit card machine

completes the check-in process, followed by a personal escort to the guest room.

The large rooms give pups of all sizes space to stretch their limbs. Floor to ceiling windows and a fluffy dog bed provide hours of entertainment to observe humanity passing by below and star-gazing above; well worth the pet's $150 price of admission. The mini-bar is stocked with sodas, water, and juice — all free, since the contemporary enclave's "home away from home" mindset shuns nickel-and-diming houseguests.

Poolside spa treatments on the rooftop sundeck channel past rock-and-roll patrons with music piped throughout the space. As the masseuse kneads tired bodies, Don Henley croons "I'm standing on a corner in Winslow, Arizona…" and helicopters fly overhead. Impromptu jam sessions on the nearby chaises are not unusual, with wanna-be musicians strumming a tune or two. No pups are permitted, but Angela from Animal People Pet Sitting will come in-house to cosset your critter.

A visit to the hotel's signature restaurant, RH, also warrants Angela's services. Chef Sebastien Archambault's authentic southern French cuisine is reminiscent of basic, high-quality dishes one may taste in Avignon or Marseille. The casual, open kitchen cooks food in full view of diners, allowing them to experience how the food is prepared. Hosts dressed in chinos and button-down shirts, sans traditional aprons or vests, blend effortlessly with the understated atmosphere.

THE LONDON WEST HOLLYWOOD
1020 San Vicente Boulevard, West Hollywood, CA 90069
(310) 854-1111 • www.thelondonwesthollywood.com ($$$)

In April, 2008, the former Bel Age hotel morphed into The London West Hollywood one block from the intersection of pulsating Sunset Boulevard and fabulous San Vicente Boulevard. Within months, the contemporary stunner was placed on Conde Nast Traveler magazine's Hot List. It typifies L.A. cool, starting with the faux park on the third floor. Hampton Court is pooch paradise for visiting dogs. With a 20 pound or less weight limit, the playground seems like Central Park to the little tykes. Adirondack chairs, set among white roses and orange trees, reinvent urban leisure.

Spacious guest rooms are home base for pet-toting travelers. Here, the pampering comes to you, whether it be a personal trainer, spa treatments, or hair styling. Complimentary calls to London, England are an extra perk, should guests have friends across the pond.

The bathroom is an experience in itself. A dual-head shower with a full-length mirror keeps guests honest at the dessert table. A waist-deep soaking tub saturates the senses with the hotel's 100% vegan essential oil skin-care products.

Gordon Ramsay, the disheveled chef on Fox's *Hell's Kitchen*, who peppers his sentences with four-letter words, lent his name to the hotel's restaurant. It's run by one of Ramsay's past apprentices, who has impeccable culinary skills, like his mentor. Cooking lessons divulging the kitchen's secret recipes are taught every other Saturday from 10a.m. to noon. Pup-sitters from Fetch will keep an eye on the pooch.

"Garbanzo," the hotel mascot, makes an appearance every Friday. The English Bulldog is hired to schmooze diva-style with "his people" for two to three hours. Cookies, with his image in frosting, are handed out to adoring fans. So "Hollywoof" !

LE MONTROSE SUITE HOTEL
900 Hammond Street, West Hollywood, CA 90069
LE PARC SUITE HOTEL
733 N. West Knoll Drive, West Hollywood, CA 90069
(310) 855-1115 • (310) 855-8888
www.lemontrose.com ($$) • www.leparcsuites.com ($$)

....

These hotels are owned by the same company, and are the closest vacationers will get to living like a local. Only one mile apart, the low-rise structures are surrounded by residential homes and apartment buildings, giving guests an opportunity to catch a glimpse of Los Angelenos' daily life. The neighborhoods ring like the United Nations with Italian, French, and Scottish brogues spoken on the sidewalks.

The hospitality is more relaxed than luxurious. Some guests stay for a night, others a month. Suites with kitchenettes and dining tables are practical for traveling families. The usual amenities are

offered, plus laundry facilities, a gym, and in-room massages. Hairy hounds smaller than a miniature horse are permitted for a $100 fee at Le Montrose, and $75 at Le Parc.

Like many siblings, the properties look similar, but have differences. Knoll Drive has 21 extra guestrooms, totaling 154. It is also eight years older. The GM's terrier, "Jackson," is the quasi-mascot whose personal business card reads, "Director of Pet Relations." Visiting pooches love his beef flavored, non-alcoholic brew Bowser Beer. Over 750 enamored fans claim the canine as their Facebook friend. With all his clout, the popular little dude should garner support in changing the hotel's "room-service only" option for pet-toting overnighters.

Le Montrose opened in 1992 before the term "boutique" became all the rage, yet it naturally conforms to the principles of such an establishment. The rooftop pool policies state "no pets" and "no food." However, salt and pepper shakers on the umbrella shaded tables and canines sharing chaises with their owners suggest otherwise. Sort of a "don't ask, don't tell" edict.

URTH CAFFÉ

8565 Melrose Avenue, West Hollywood, CA 90069

(310) 659-0628 • www.urthcaffe.com ($$)

Gone are the days when only Birkenstock-clad beatniks ate garbanzo beans, alfalfa sprouts and eggplant lasagna. The Manolo Blahnik set has boned up on chemical-free produce and now can't get enough. Large crowds wait out front to get a table at this organic

oracle. Established in 1989 as a coffee company, Urth has blossomed into a full restaurant with four Los Angeles locations (Beverly Hills, Santa Monica and Downtown). Breakfast pastries are made in-house and the fresh fruit salad is cut to order. Patio camaraderie with fellow pooch-packing patrons is from 6:30 a.m. till 11:30 p.m.. The boys of HBO's *Entourage* hang out at the 90210 locale. Delivery is available. To-go cups are made from a compostable, natural material derived from corn.

SUR RESTAURANT

606 North Robertson Boulevard, West Hollywood, CA 90069

(310) 289-2824 • www.sur-restaurant.com ($$)

Where trendy Melrose Avenue meets hip Robertson Boulevard, this unobtrusive restaurant hums with the convivial banter of L.A.'s beautiful people. It's quite a celebrity hangout, luring Madonna with the Chilean Sea Bass, and Vanessa Williams by way of the Ahi Tuna. An elegant indoor/outdoor patio, secluded by billowing white curtains, is washed in candlelight with only fresh blooms and leafy plants supplying color. Pups curl up on the polished floor underneath linen-draped tables. The inside is more lavish, with velvet upholstery, chandeliers, and a grandiose Buddha statue greeting diners. The exotic flair of Sur's décor and cuisine is a blending of the four owners, who hail from Argentina, France, and Great Britain. Endive and Nicoise Salad, Shrimp Risotto with Sweet Peas, and Rib Eye Steak Smothered in Five-Peppercorn Red Wine Sauce, evoke their unique backgrounds.

TENDER GREENS

8759 Santa Monica Boulevard, West Hollywood, CA 90069
(310) 358-1919 • www.tendergreensfood.com ($$)
....

This cool corner eatery on a bustling WeHo street was born and bred on the concept that organic, farm-fresh produce, range-raised meat, and Pacific-caught tuna is not a luxury, but a healthy necessity. The interior is as unfettered as the food – clean and sleek with no unnecessary additives. From carnivores to vegans, marinated steak to Ferro wheat salad, there's a dish for every taste. Business professionals stop in for lunch and vacationers linger over freshly made desserts. Patrons order and pay inside, and a server delivers the food to the pooch-friendly outside tables.

SADDLE RANCH CHOP HOUSE

8371 West Sunset Boulevard, West Hollywood, CA 90069
(323) 656-2007 • www.srrestaurants.com ($$$)
....

With a menu the length of a short story, diners can reach their daily caloric intake after one meal. The "ride-'em-cowboy" motif is a bit out of character for the otherwise ultra chic Sunset Strip. It's more like a Hollywood set, with guests playing the leading roles. In true Texas fashion, dishes are the size of wagon wheels and cocktails are colossal. People-watching on the front deck is worthy of an admission

price, but there is none. Shuffle the pooch under the table, and dive into signature dishes of Sweet Potato Pancakes, Hacienda Salad, or Hand-Toasted S'mores at one of the campfire pits. They're open 365 days a year, should one feel inclined to ride the mechanical bull on Christmas Day.

TOAST BAKERY CAFÉ
8221 West Third Street, Los Angeles, CA 90048
(323) 655-5018 • www.toastbakerycafe.net ($)

....

The aromas of percolating coffee and griddle sweets start to fill the air around 7:30 a.m. Lots of sidewalk tables splayed on both sides of the corner building have ample room for dogs and diners. Pasta with Scrambled Eggs and Turkey Sausage scores high on the delicious scale. Not to be outdone is the Shakshuka – slow roasted tomatoes, peppers and garlic stew capped with fried eggs. Hungry patrons wanting soup, salad and "burgs" keep the servers hopping till 10 p.m..

YOGURT STOP
8803 Santa Monica Boulevard, West Hollywood, CA 90069
(310) 652-6830 • www.yogurtstop.net ($)

....

Serving yogurt until two in the morning indicates this isn't a kid-die's parlor. The sweetery, with only one location in the world, has been ranked #1 Frozen Yogurt in L.A. by Los Angeles magazine. Pump-it-yourself dispensers coil creamy delights titled "Peaches Loves Pageants," "I Like Boys-And-Berrys," and the owner's defer-ence to the surrounding GLBT neighborhood, "Lesbonic Tonic." "I'm Coming Out Cake Batter" is the hands-down favorite. One lick will suffice for pups' sensitive digestive tracts, but with ongoing name and recipe contests, Fido may get a flavor in the future.

Play

WELLS FARGO BANK
8571 Santa Monica Boulevard, West Hollywood, CA 90069
(310) 855-7140 • www.wellsfargo.com
....

For those who want Fido to pull his share of the financial load, your wish has been answered. WeHo's Wells Fargo has taken humanization of animals to the next level. With $25 and the parents' social security number, canines can open a savings account. No ATM card is issued, just a statement with the lovable-lug's name.

While an exact count of canine customers can't be divulged for privacy reasons, suffice it to say lots of pooches have placed their "paw prints" on the dotted line. Spending decisions fall on the owner, safeguarding against fanatical obsessions with bling collars or "puptinis." The money is often used for unforeseen veterinary bills, vacations at pet-friendly hotels and countless other Rover-related bills. The "Boys Town" branch is the sole participant in helping Fido stockpile bones for a rainy day; a clever choice with its estimated 1,000 dogs per square mile.

MOVIE STAR HOMES TOUR
Maps sold on street corners along Sunset Boulevard, between Highland Avenue and Fairfax Avenue or can be purchased online www.MovieStarHomesTour.com ($)
....

Nothing says "Tinseltown Vaca" more than a self-guided driving tour of the movie stars' homes. Crank open the sunroof, grab your four-legged co-pilot, and head for the hills…Hollywood Hills. Most celebrity cribs can be accessed from Sunset Boulevard. The

mega famous are on the list: TomKat, Jennifer Lopez, Simon Cowell, Drew Barrymore, Tori Spelling, and Springsteen. Hef's Playboy Mansion, the former Beverly Hillbillies' abode and Ray Charles' digs before his demise, add variety to the 500-name directory. See where the magic happens at Paramount Studios and 20th Century Fox. Traverse city streets to NBC Studio and CBS Television City. Those with an affinity for the morbid will want to get the L.A. Crime Scenes map, locating the O.J. Simpson double murder site and the Menendez brothers' home. For the faint-at-heart, best to skip the gruesomeness; instead, check out the stars on the Hollywood Walk of Fame.

LAKE HOLLYWOOD PARK

3160 Canyon Lake Drive, Los Angeles, CA 90027
(323) 913-4688 • www.laparks.org
....

Because of the park's hushed whereabouts, it's known as L.A.'s "underground" dog park. Its proximity below the famous Hollywood sign grants unparalleled photo-ops. The iconic letters were originally built in 1923 as a billboard for "Hollywoodland" housing development. They were illuminated with 4,000 light bulbs, which sequentially blinked "Holly," "Wood," "Land," ending with a huge period. In the 1970s the landmark had lost its last four letters and was in need of repair. Hugh Heffner hosted a fundraiser, auctioning off individual characters. Rock star Alice Cooper bought an "O," cowboy Gene Autry purchased an "L," and Andy Williams sponsored the "W." Other donors acquired the remaining six symbols, restoring the emblem to its former glory. Pups visiting the park should be harnessed, but due to the Park Ranger's infrequent visits, it's pseudo leash-free. Benches, picnic tables and a children's playground enhance the restful, clean setting.

RUNYON CANYON
2000 North Fuller Avenue, Los Angles, CA 90046
(213) 485-5572 • www.laparks.org
....

A 130-acre hiatus from the cement city, "Run," as locals refer to it, is only two blocks from the hustle-and-bustle of Holly-wood. An honor table at the entrance trusts hikers to place $1 in the jar in return for granola bars, water, and bananas. The dog treats are free. Wild chaparral and drought-resistant trees flourish in the sunny, hot canyon. Steep climbs to the ridge are rewarded with stellar views of the Griffith Observatory and a gentle trail walk back down. Over half the park allows pooches to be off-leash, but beware if your pup isn't fond of romping with other canines, as there are throngs  of them, some with no manners. Celebrity sightings are common, although they're harder to recognize wearing ball caps and shades.

GRIFFITH PARK
4730 Crystal Springs Drive
(Los Feliz Boulevard to the south and Ventura Freeway to the north)
Los Angeles, CA 90027
(323) 913-4688 (Park Ranger Station)
www.laparks.org ($ Miniature Train) • www.angeles.sierraclub.org
....

Griffith is the largest urban park in America, covering 4,210 acres – the equivalent of five square miles. The woodsy playground was

donated in 1896 by a wealthy gold mine speculator, Griffith J. Griffith (yes, that's correct), whose trust fund monies built a Greek theater and observatory in the park after his death. A large portion of the pooch paradise remains unchanged today. Rover can ride the rails on an open air miniature train, romp in the off-leash dog sanctuary (on North Zoo Drive), or take a moonlight hike sponsored by the Sierra Club.

LA DOG WORKS

1014 North Highland Avenue, Los Angeles, CA 90038
(323) 461-5151 • www.ladogworks.com ($$$)
....

Head out to the Getty Museum, L.A. Symphony, or a night on the town and leave the pupster at this canine country club for a romping good time of his own. Andrew Rosenthal, the president and alpha male, offers 24 hour daycare for furry scions vacationing with their parents. Drop them off and pick them up whenever you want. Shuttle service is also available. A brief temperament evaluation and proof of vaccinations is required prior to Fido's jubilant playtime in the 2,500-square-foot indoor dog park. A certified staff of 40 keeps the facility immaculate, disinfecting regularly with organic enzymes. Fashionistas may opt for a pawdicure, hair color, or a massage in the Zen Den.

SUNSET PLAZA

West Sunset Boulevard, between Alta Loma Road and Horn Avenue
West Hollywood, CA 90069
www.visitwesthollywood.com • www.lepetitfour.net
www.zadig-et-voltaire.com • www.cravingsrestaurant.com
....

Two blocks of boutiques and bistros rest amid Sunset Strip's high-rise buildings clad in advertisements with thin blondes wearing tight jeans. Both sides of the street boast fashion's biggest names alongside up-and-coming designers. Retailers are on top of their game to please the area's pervasive "me" mentality. Zadig & Voltaire's hip clothing has two U.S. locations, here and in N.Y.C.. Code C exhibits local and international stylists' collections, many worn by Heidi Klum and Kate Hudson. Pooches and their loved ones can check out the lively café scene at Cravings

restaurant or Le Petit Four. Free parking is behind the storefronts or meters take credit cards, so shop till you hit your credit limit.

AVENUES OF ART & DESIGN

Melrose Avenue, Beverly Boulevard and Robertson Boulevard
West Hollywood, CA 90069
(310) 289-2534
www.avenuesartdesign.com • www.visitwesthollywood.com/podcasts
www.makeupmandy.com • www.positanosandalo.com
....

A shopper's mecca, this pedestrian-friendly design district has over three hundred art galleries, antique stores, flagship boutiques, furniture showrooms, and eateries. A ten-minute walking tour podcast is available online, or pick up a map from the hotel concierge. Transformed from its penumbra of obscurity into a wholesale quarter, it has blossomed as a high-end retail fashion destination where celebrities shop daily. Stella McCartney's west coast atelier and Armani Casa display masterpieces. Makeup Mandy Eyelash Bar extends peeper-tresses as the pooch looks on. Positano Sandalos creates customized Italian Caprisian sandals. Choose the heel, color, and accessories, then return in an hour to pick up the finished product, complete with personalized engraving.

SANTA MONICA BOULEVARD
La Brea Avenue to Doheny Drive, West Hollywood, CA 90069
www.visitwesthollywood.com

....

"The Boulevard" runs from Hollywood to Santa Monica, with WeHo's 1.9-mile portion being the most diverse. Route 66 signage dots the thoroughfare, which is part of America's mother road. The lively district has both ethnic and lifestyle representation, with a Russian community and a large gay population. The west end is nicknamed "Boys Town." Rainbow flags decorate the grassy median. Eclectic shops, clubs, and cafes line the sidewalks, where a short stroll reveals no less than a dozen fur-children out for a walk with their parents. The place hops every evening, but especially on October 31st when the world's largest adult outdoor Halloween event packs the street.

Veterinarian

TLC PET MEDICAL CENTERS AND
LOS ANGELES VETERINARY SPECIALISTS
8725 Santa Monica Boulevard, West Hollywood, CA 90069
(310) 859-4852 • www.tlcvet.com
24 Hour Emergency and appointments daily

....

Stay

THE LANGHAM HUNTINGTON HOTEL & SPA
1401 South Oak Knoll Avenue, Pasadena, CA 91106
(626) 568-3900 • www.langhamhotels.com ($$$)
....

Few hotels truly look like their glossy brochures; The Langham does. This beauty impresses even well-heeled travelers who have slumbered at innumerable world-class resorts. Set on 23-acres among an elegant neighborhood with mini-mansions, the 1907 building's present day revitalization still offers glimpses of its past life as the Hotel Wentworth.

The entryway's lily signature scent and clean crisp décor pair perfectly. Ruby red amaryllis flowers and violet hydrangea blooms are the only source of color. Wide corridors – a throwback from the era of hefty steamer trunks – encircle an interior courtyard off the lobby, with a pond and tables for enjoying a good book with pooches.

Permissible pup size is 40 pounds or less, and the cost $125. Not only a dog bed, but a matching pillow and blanket wait in the room. Add bottled water and bowls, and the result is one spoiled dawg. People's amenities rival their furry friends, with down comforters smothered in soft linens and a plate of chocolates with

chilled pink lemonade at the evening turndown. Don't worry about forgotten toiletries. A brown leather box on the bathroom counter is neatly packed with everything you could need. Of the hotel's 380 rooms, the ground floor's proximity to Horseshoe Garden makes it easier for Fido to be footloose and fancy free. Private terraces make it optimal for in-room dining with pets.

One of The Langham's pride and joy features is Picture Bridge, which connects the main building to a dozen cottages and tennis courts. The covered footpath constructed of redwood offers views of the pool and Japanese Garden below. Painted murals on the rooftop gables depict 41 scenes of California. Conceived by Frank Moore in 1932, the budding artist was paid $10 per scene and all the food he and his wife could eat. Poet Donald Blanding's lyrical verses are posted along the beams.

Another nod to the past is an antique railroad bell in the aforementioned courtyard. Every evening at 7:05 p.m., it is rung seven times to mark the Change Of Day and to pay tribute to a previous owner and hotel's namesake, Henry Huntington, who played a vital role in the development of Southern California railroads. The tradition was initiated in 1865, and is now combined with dimming the lobby lights and luminating candles. Ironically, throughout the day, guests will periodically hear the faint whistle of far-off passing Amtrak trains.

Kibble

MADELEINES RESTAURANT AND WINE BISTRO
1030 East Green Street, Pasadena, CA 91106
(626) 440-7087 • www.madeleinesrestaurant.com ($$$$)
....

As with many French influenced establishments, the atmosphere at Madeleines is divinely elegant without being ostentatious. The food

follows suit. Impeccable service is extended to nine tables on the front patio where dogs can dine. Each selection is as good as the next, whether it's Pan-Seared Duck Breast with a Blueberry Port Reduction or Black Cod resting on Root Vegetable Puree. A more casual list of options pleases lunch palates. Either menu pairs well with the exceptional wine selection, showcasing White Burgundy, Viognier, and numerous other varietals from western and eastern Europe and the U.S.A.

Play

LACY PARK
1485 Virginia Road, San Marino, CA 91108
(626) 300-0790 • www.cityofsanmarino.org ($ weekend admission)
....

The immaculate 26.5 acres looks more like Philadelphia's Longwood Gardens than a neighborhood park. It's touted as a horticul-

tural showcase with its diverse plant species and approximately 900 trees, most planted nearly 100 years ago. Complimentary guides listing the different genera are at the entrance. Bucolic lawns offer space for Buster to bound and circular walkways provide terra firma for buggy-pushing mamas. A George Patton military memorial proudly flies flags of the Navy, Army, Air Force, Marines and Coast Guard. The Historical Society headquarters reside on the north side. As with most of the Pasadena area, Henry Huntington played a large role in bringing the peaceful hamlet to fruition with his donations many years ago. Today, due to its popularity on weekends, admission is charged. Weekdays are free.

URBAN SHOPPING ADVENTURES
846 South Broadway #705, Los Angeles, CA 90014
(213) 683-9715 • www.urbanshoppingadventures.com

No one knows Pasadena's fashion scene like Christine Silvestri, owner and style maven of Urban Shopping Adventures. Silvestri personally escorts clients and their canines around San Gabriel Valley's Old

Pasadena with J. Crew, Kenneth Cole and other hip boutiques lining its streets. Antique hunting at upscale Paseo Colorado district is another fun choice. A five-minute Shopping School starts all the two-and-a-half-hour tours; shopping bags with area maps, a beverage, and snack bar are provided. Under Silvestri's tutelage, customers find items for their wardrobes and jewelry boxes without rendering themselves penniless. Many merchants offer discounts to the tour participants.

SOUTH LAKE AVENUE
Lake Avenue, between Colorado Boulevard and California Boulevard
Pasadena, CA 91101
(626) 792-1259 (South Lake Business Association)
www.southlakeavenue.com
www.chamkoreanbistro.com • www.greenstreetrestaurant.com

"South Lake" is ten blocks of Pottery Barn, Willams-Sonoma, Macy's, Talbots and the like, with cafes sprinkled along the hip corridor. Pups and patrons spend hours amid the iconic stores, weaving throughout adjacent streets to sample culinary treats such as

LA – PASADENA

CHAM Korean Bistro's Kimchi and Persimmon Salad, or Green Street Restaurant's more traditional fare. The South Lake Business Association hosts Wine and Food Festivals, children's activities, and live music throughout the year.

Veterinarian

ANIMAL EMERGENCY CLINIC OF PASADENA
2121 East Foothill Boulevard, Pasadena, CA 91107
(626) 564-0704
Open Monday thru Friday 6 p.m. till 8 a.m.
Saturday from 12 noon until Monday at 8 a.m.
....

FOOTHILL VETERINARY HOSPITAL
2204 East Foothill Boulevard, Pasadena, CA 91107
(626) 792-1187 • www.foothillvet.com
Open Monday thru Friday 7:30 a.m. until 6:30 p.m.
Saturday 8 a.m. until 1 p.m., Sunday closed
....

My goal in life is to be as good of a person
my dog already thinks I am.

– Unknown

Life doesn't get much better than in Santa Barbara, "The American Riviera." Residents have it all – a burgeoning wine country, quaint downtown shops, delicious dining, and flower-festooned inns nestled among the Santa Ynez mountains. A higher standard of living is the norm here. That goes for pooches, too. Carivintas Winery offers customized labels with a photo of the proud parent's canine. From the Mission to the Pier, dogs join in the fun. The Chumash Indians were the first to become enamored with the idyllic locale, forging an open road for future wanderlusts. Five centuries later, people are still captivated by its beauty, class, and status as the perfect vacation destination. One visit is all it takes.

SANTA BARBARA

SANTA BARBARA • OJAI

Santa Maria

Santa Barbara

Los Alamos

Los Olivos

Santa Ynez

Lompoc

San Ysidro Ranch

Ojai Valley
Inn and Spa

101

Santa Barbara

Montecito

Oja

Fess Parker's
Doubletree Resort

Four Seasons
Resort The Biltmore

Canary Hotel

Oxna

Stay

FESS PARKER'S DOUBLETREE RESORT

633 East Cabrillo Boulevard, Santa Barbara, CA 93103 🐕 🐕 🐕 🐕

(805) 564-4333 • www.fpdtr.com ($$$)

....

It should come as no surprise that a hotel opened by Fess Parker, a.k.a. "Daniel Boone," welcomes doggies with open arms. The resort does hospitality the old-fashioned way — warm, friendly, and doesn't try to be something it's not. It's a place where kin come from the Midwest for weddings and the Bible is still place in bed-side table drawers.

The glass atrium lobby grants views of the Plaza Del Sol courtyard and the Channel Islands twenty-two miles out to sea. Rosy-cheeked receptionists greet guests with warm chocolate chip cookies, and pooches get a treat, too. Pet guidelines are reviewed: no weight re-striction, a $25 per night charge, food bowls upon request, "paw"-riffic and "purr"-riffic pet menus for in-room dining, "Pet Post" locations with waste "Mutt mitts," and directions to designated canine rooms.

The Azalea building is pup central, providing access to lawns, a promenade stretching the length of the 24-acre property, and Santa Barbara's three-mile waterfront path at the Harbor. The ample rooms, with 1970s décor of pineapple lamps and shinny wood throughout, sit a stone's-throw from the Pacific. If there's an influx of furry friends, the adjacent Bougainvillea and Eucalyptus guest room complexes will house the overflow. The gift shop – more like a general store – sells pup toys, leashes, collars, and any belongings one may have not packed.

Varietals produced by the Fess Parker Winery located 35 miles inland are featured Friday and Saturday evenings from 5 p.m. to 7 p.m. in the lobby. Ashley's Chardonnay – named for Parker's daughter, who co-runs the winery with her brother, Eli – is one vintage on a list comprised of pinot noirs and syrah's. The convivial two and four-legged crowd mingle easily.

Dinner and lunch are served on the casual Barra Los Arcos terrace. Romantic two-tops are huddled by the fireplace, or large tables oblige any size family. Breakfast grab-and-go snacks are sold at the Java Del Mar espresso bar.

SAN YSIDRO RANCH
900 San Ysidro Lane, Santa Barbara, CA 93108
(805) 565-1700 • www.sanysidroranch.com ($$$$)

Every dog has his day, and for the lucky ones it's a vacation with the parents at San Ysidro Ranch. This property has the same expansive views of the Santa Ynez Mountains, and identical sagebrush scented air as Montecitos famous resident, Oprah. Over 500-acres of pampered, raw nature in the foothills cocoon 41 rooms, cottages, and suites. Brain-jostling beauty starts upon arrival with a verdant cobblestone lane leading to the registration hacienda, and sprays of bougainvillea draped over the front porch. There are two sign-in books, one for guests and the other for visiting pets, which sometimes is a puddie-tat or a lizard. The pet-friendly tradition began decades ago when Senator Alvin Weingand and his Dachshunds frequented the property. A weathervane with a cut-out of the breed twirls atop the adjacent Old Adobe building commemorating his buddies.

Formerly a citrus farm, the elegant guest ranch has come a long way over the past century to it's position of "America's Best Hotel" by Forbes Traveler. A picture-postcard scene is around every corner as visitors head

to their private quarters. Stepping-stone paths meander through a sea of wildflowers, water trickles into a lily pond, and rose-covered arbors shade benches. Eighteen free-standing bungalows with private patios accommo-date pups. Great-Dane-sized beds and SYR branded food bowls are supplied, as well as a toy from Ty Warner of Beanie Babies fame, who owns the estate. Fido's fee for all this is $100 per stay.

The ranch's 17 miles of hiking trails, ranging from a gentle walk to a waterfall, or the more rigorous four-mile jaunt up Montecito Peak, is enough to tucker out even the squirmiest of pooches. Their reward: a 30-minute Mutt Massage to soothe tired limbs and an eight-ounce sirloin burger from the pet menu. Afterwards, mosey over to the hacienda's patio or library for a cocktail. The bartender's VSOP, Cointreau, and lime juice concoction is named after the ranch cat, "Bentley." Back to the cottage for dining, as this is the only option with pets. An appreciated rule, since the digs are so wonderful.

FOUR SEASONS RESORT THE BILTMORE SANTA BARBARA
1260 Channel Drive, Santa Barbara, CA 93108
(805) 969-2261 • www.fourseasons.com/santabarbara ($$$$)

The beachfront 1927 Spanish Colonial landmark is another one of Ty Warner's properties in elite Montecito. The self-made, multi-billionaire accumulated his fortune in the 1990s with the Beanie Babies collecting craze. At the height of the stuffed toys' popularity, certain cuddly animals sold for $5,000 on the secondary market, prompting enterprising individuals to purchase several at their original price of $5 as an investment. At the time, Ty, Inc. had larger sales than Hasbro and Mattel combined. Warner plowed his profits into real estate and hotels in New York, Hawaii, Mexico and California, as well as millions of dollars into philanthropic organizations such as the Sea Center in Santa Barbara.

Upon acquiring the Four Seasons Biltmore in 2000, Warner started a $60 million makeover of the 207 guest rooms, keeping the architectural integrity, but updating amenities. More importantly, regal pup beds embossed with the chain's tree logo and doggie dishes were placed in the pooch-friendly cottages. The pet fee is zero, and the sky's the limit for weight. Petable patrons love Monte Vista

Lawn on the east side of the inn's 27-acres. A nine-hole putting green and plenty of space to toss a Frisbee provides entertainment for the whole family. Have a picnic basket delivered with sandwiches, cookies, and wine. Every Tuesday at 11a.m. a one-hour botanical tour, guided by the jovial grounds manager, encourages guests to explore the remaining acreage. The concierge has a map listing the plants, should guests desire meandering on their own.

Butterfly Beach, directly in front of the hotel entrance, is well-used by residents. Rules state pups must be leashed, but cavorting dogs indicate otherwise. The offshore oil wells deposit tar and grease on the sand, so regulars know to keep their eyes peeled. Another option is to leave Bowser in the air-conditioned room with a pet-sitter and try out the $65 million Coral Casino Beach and Cabana Club across the street, overlooking Butterfly's sandy seafront. Admission is free for hotel guests. A pool, jacuzzi, steam rooms, workout classes and two restaurants will gobble up an entire day. The walls are decorated with historic black-and-white photos taken over the past 50 years by Hal Boucher. The octogenarian is still a shutterbug and offers to immortalize vacations with a framed portrait – pooch and all.

CANARY HOTEL
31 West Carrillo Street, Santa Barbara, CA 93101 🐕🐕🐕🐕
(805) 884-0300 • www.canarysantabarbara.com ($$)

....

Upon pulling under the Porte-Cochere, guests are transported to the Spanish Canary Islands off the coast of Africa, for which the hotel is named. Moorish tiles with geometric patterns and vibrant hanging tapestries decorate

the lobby walls. Dark oak furniture on polished terrazzo floors complete the European ambiance.

The Canary Islands are named after large dogs called Presa Canario, found living on these Atlantic Ocean islets. With this in mind, the downtown Santa Barbara hotel has initiated Club Canario for visiting pooches. The hotel's namesake canines usually reach 90 to100 pounds, so it's only right that there's no weight restriction for vacationing pups. There is an $85 fee. A goodie bag filled with treats, a collar tag with the hotel's yellow birdie logo, and a grooming kit complete with oatmeal shampoo and Fur Breeze spa mist is presented at check-in. An accompanying pamphlet lists dog-sitters, walkers, and washers. Housekeeping delivers beds and bowls.

The 97 room urban hideaway graces The Small Leading Hotels of the World list. It stands on a busy city corner, just one block off State Street and three blocks from the beach. Interior designer Michael S. Smith covered hallway walls in teal burlap and framed embroidered textiles. Simple "nesting" quarters with walnut canopy beds and upholstered lounge chairs overlook the street action below. Coast, the first floor restaurant, cannot serve pups, but the same nutritious meals can be delivered to the hotel's vestibule den. So, in the words of the pet-program brochure….Come. Sit. Stay.

OJAI VALLEY INN AND SPA
905 Country Club Road, Ojai, CA 93023
(800) 422-OJAI (6524) • (805) 646-1111 • www.ojairesort.com ($$$$)

The peaceful valley of Ojai (pronounced "oh hi") rests in the cupped hands of the Topa Topa Mountains. Its name is credited to the original inhabitants, the Chumash Indians, and translates as "moons nest" in their native language. Located 35 miles southeast of Santa Barbara, the artsy village is home to roughly 10,000 people, as well as its namesake Five Diamond Inn and Spa.

A $90 million renovation enlarged 308 guestrooms and introduced a 33,000-square-foot spa, catapulting the 220-acre retreat onto Conde Nast Travelers' Gold List. Pets of any size stay in the Shangri-La building, with a charge of $100 or $150, depending on whether it's a suite or room. A pet brochure given at check-in provides phone numbers of walkers and sitters, an in-room mutt menu, and a mobile groomer.

Activities play a leading role at the Inn. The par-70 golf course stacks up as a worthy challenge for the best of players. During the tough 6,292 yards, redemption enters the links in the form of a snack cart supplying brewskis and munchies.

Spa Ojai's Artist Cottage and Apothecary classes are a must. Gifted Artist in Residence Renate Collins and her team are truly emblematic of Ojai's unique offerings. Collins' masterpieces hang throughout the 1,200-foot sunlit studio beneath a centuries-old oak tree. The calming atmosphere coaxes guests' creative juices to alter a piece of silk into a vibrant scarf. Create a Personal Mandala, which

is used in Hinduism as a meditation tool. The circular, painted design represents the past, present, and future, revealing one's purpose and direction. Another pursuit is custom blending with essential oils. A quick sniff of a dozen or so scents lets intuition choose a personal perfume.

The cottage and spa are Freedom Zones, meaning free from smoking, pets, cell phones and young children, so keep the sitter on speed-dial. Make amends by taking the pooch on an organized 50 minute morning fitness hike, afternoon nature walk, or a game of "fetch" on Recreation Field beside the Inn's veggie garden.

The recipient of those fresh edibles is the Oak Grill, where Chef Jamie West works his magic. Savory lunches and dinners are served to pups and people on the upper terrace. Adjacent Jimmy's Pub serves brick oven pizzas, boutique beers and California wines, reserving one outside table for canines.

EMILIO'S RISTORANTE
324 West Cabrillo Boulevard, Santa Barbara, CA 93101
(805) 966-4426 • www.emiliosrestaurant.com ($$$)
....

The Italian cuisine at this dinner-only restaurant has garnered visits from celebrity chefs Todd English and Lidia Bastianch. The owner makes friends easily with the patrons; must be his background as a carnival worker. Weekdays offer a three-course prix fixe menu with choices of Pesto Fettuccini and Mascarpone Ravioli as main dishes. Weekends, a la carte fare tempts with Ahi Tuna Cones and Slow-Roasted Pork. Doggie diners eat at waterfront tables and watch boats bob in the marina.

TUPELO JUNCTION CAFÉ
1218 State Street, Santa Barbara, CA 93101
(805) 899-3100 • www.tupelojunction.com ($$$)

....

The bounty from local farms supplies this State Street restaurant
with a healthy twist on Southern cooking. Their Fried Chicken on
a Bed of Salad Greens is the house specialty. Pumpkin seeds and a
lemony-herb buttermilk dressing help lighten up the dish. Shrimp
and Scallops with Cheddar Jalapeno Grits and Lobster Creole
Butter is delicious, as well. These variations on traditional recipes
prompted Bon Appetite magazine to exclaim "Do not miss" when
in Santa Barbara. Pooches' favorite? A sidewalk table and "Hush-
puppies," of course.

ANDERSEN'S DANISH RESTAURANT AND BAKERY
1106 State Street, Santa Barbara, CA 93101
(805) 962-5085 • www.andersenssantabarbara.com ($$)

....

The Danes have brought pork schnitzel and apple strudel to Santa
Barbara. The cutlets and pastries have been served daily for 30
years, along with
a gluttony of
culinary delights.
Snag a sidewalk
table with room
for the *hund* to curl
up underneath,
and decide which
heaping platter you
must sample. The
Ham, Cheese, and
Liver Pate sand-
wich is considered
a European break-

fast. High Tea is served from 2 p.m. to 5 p.m.. The chocolate fondue paired with a variety of red wines is par excellence. A Havarti
Cheese Sandwich washed down with Koenig Pilsner is a simpler
palate pleaser.

OUR DAILY BREAD BAKERY & CAFÉ

831 Santa Barbara Street, Santa Barbara, CA 93101

(805) 966-3894 • www.ourdailybread.net ($)

....

Sometimes the most delicious food comes from the most casual eateries. That's the case at this wholesome café located on a quiet street off the beaten path. Meals are prepared the way Mother Nature intended – wholesome and unmodified. Muffins are baked daily with corn and raspberries, as is their Tomato Gorgonzola Foccacia. Multigrain paninis overflow with tri-tip or grilled veggies. Order at the counter, and a server will deliver the goodies and a bowl of water for Fido to the sidewalk tables. Breakfast and lunch only, and it's closed on Sunday; as the Lord's Prayer says, "give us this day Our Daily Bread."

PANINO

834 Santa Barbara Street, Santa Barbara, CA 93101

(805) 963-3700 • www.paninoinc.com ($)

....

Located across the street from Our Daily Bread, this laid-back café has scored Santa Barbara News-Press' "Winner of the Best Sandwiches" four years straight. A bite into the Curried Chicken Salad reveals chunks of poultry, not shreds. Albacore tuna with artichoke hearts and kalamata olives merge perfectly between whole wheat slices. The Roasted Turkey and Imported Genoa Salami Combo ranks high with the customers, as well as pooches lucky enough to snag a bite. Caprese Insalada is a tasty add-on. Panino is open Monday thru Saturday, 10a.m. to 4p.m. and Sunday, 11a.m. to 3p.m..

MOVINO WINE BAR AND GALLERY
308 East Ojai Avenue, Ojai, CA 93023
(805) 646-1555 • www.movinowinebar.com ($$)
....

The name of the restaurant is a combination of owner Suzy Johlfs's nickname, "Mo" and the ancient European's moniker for wine, "vino." The fruit of the grape is in numerous meals. Chardonnay spikes the Caesar salad dressing and Grand Marnier strawberry sauce is drizzled over baked brie. All the dishes are en-

hanced by the menu's suggested central coast wine pairings. Artists' paintings and sculptures are featured and available for sale. The silky tones of live music three nights a week entertain patio diners and their four-legged companions.

Play

STEARNS WHARF

Intersection of State Street and West Cabrillo Boulevard
Santa Barbara, CA 93101
(805) 564-5530 (Santa Barbara Waterfront Administration)
www.stearnswharf.org • www.sbparks.org (Arroyo Burro Beach)
www.sbshellfishco.com ($) • www.captdon.com ($)
....

A gurgling fountain with three cast-iron dolphins signifies the entrance of the oldest operating wharf on the West Coast. Pelicans and sea gulls fly overhead as leashed dogs and their owners take in the fresh salt air. Pedestrians walk on the right side of the wooden-plank pier; cars drive on the left. Fill a basket with goodies and eat at the picnic tables located on the end, or order take-out from the adjacent Santa Barbara Shell Fish Company. Stearns Wharf Bait and Tackle helps you catch the "big one." Captain Don's Pirate Cruises welcome two and four-legged mateys. The beach directly underneath the pier doesn't allow K9s, but three miles north is pet-friendly Arroyo Burro Beach. One caveat; tar and grease dregs from the off-shore oil wells are deposited onto the sand.

RED TILE WALKING TOUR

Within the square blocks of Anapamu Street, State Street,
De la Guerra Street, and Santa Barbara Street
Santa Barbara, CA 93101
(805) 966-9222 (Santa Barbara Conference & Visitors Bureau)
www.santabarbaraca.com/podcasts
....

Soak up the sun on a 12 block, self-guided walking tour through downtown, showcasing the Spanish-Revival and Moorish architecture and its red tile roofs. Pass an 18th century military outpost depicting how the early settlers lived, and the city's oldest adobe, Santiago de la Guerra, which dates to 1812. Chumash Indian artifacts fill the Santa Barbara Historical Museum. The Visitors Bureau website provides a downloadable map and video podcast narrated by "Seinfeld's" John O'Hurley, an avid dog lover.

OLD MISSION SANTA BARBARA
2201 Laguna Street, Santa Barbara, CA 93105
(805) 682-4713 • www.santabarbaramission.org ($ Admission & Tour)
....

Established in 1786 by Spanish Franciscans, this beauty was the tenth of the twenty-one missions built in California. Subsequent years brought destruction of the adobe structure from earthquakes

and fire, requiring the townspeople to rebuild numerous times. Today's Neo-Classical stone mission exhibits Baroque art and statues saved from the earlier churches. A large, active parish collaborates with the Franciscan Friars, who live on the grounds,

to keep the church active in the community. Pups and parents can play on the front lawn, mosey around the rose garden park across the street, or browse the gift shop, but no admission into the shrine or its museum for pooches.

SANTA YNEZ WINE COUNTRY
Personal Tours, Ltd., P.O. Box 60109, Santa Barbara, CA 93160
(805) 685-0552 • www.personaltoursltd.com ($$$)
www.sbcountywines.com
....

Dogs do not qualify as designated drivers, so booking a chauffer to the wine country is paramount. Personal Tours guides meet at the hotel and drive clients' vehicles to the valley's 70-plus wineries,

45 miles east of Santa Barbara. The itinerary is custom designed, allowing passengers to choose their desired vineyards, or shop boutiques, visit a lavender farm, or even check out an exotic animal ranch. Retracing the route of the indie film, *Sideways*, is fun. Due to the rural nature, most chateaus own mascot mutts that are territorial over their turf, making it necessary for visiting pooches to stay in the car. Drivers charge by the hour, with a five-hour minimum on weekends. Those wanting to stay closer to "home" can visit the numerous tasting rooms sprinkled throughout downtown Santa Barbara.

OJAI VALLEY MUSEUM HISTORICAL WALKING TOUR

130 West Ojai Avenue, Ojai, CA 93023

(805) 640-1390 • www.ojaivalleymuseum.org ($)

Saturdays 10:30 a.m.

Walk on the same streets as the city's benefactor, glass tycoon Edward Libbey, whose cohesive efforts in the early 1900s took Ojai from a dusty outpost to the upscale area it is today. The one-mile tour takes an hour, with lots of stops for pups to rest. Amble past the Old Mission-Style Church, the town's first brick schoolhouse, and Libbey Park, home to the old jail and Libbey Bowl outdoor amphitheater. With a small group size of 12 to15 people, it's advisable to make reservations.

OJAI VALLEY TRAIL AND LOS PADRES NATIONAL FOREST TRAILS

Ojai, CA 93023

(805) 646-8126 • www.ojaichamber.org

The Ojai Valley Trail is a nine-and-a-half mile paved road for leashed pooches and people to enjoy. It parallels two-lane Highway 33. A post-and-rail fence separates a wood-chipped horse path from the asphalt footpath. The road starts on Fox Street in Ojai and ends at Forest Park on the border of Ventura. Bike, walk, or jog among mature oak trees and meet "townies" who use the path daily, sometimes sauntering with their pet pot bellied pigs.

A more rustic route is The Los Padres National Forest, which surrounds Ojai valley and sustains 195 miles of dirt trails. The Chamber of Commerce website sells a map highlighting the length

and difficulty level of 24 routes. Some are close to the village and pet-friendly for furry hikers on a leash.

Fetch

MONTECITO VILLAGE AND COAST VILLAGE
East Valley Road and Coast Village Road, Montecito, CA 93108
www.santabarbaraca.com • www.maisonkinc.com
www.livinggreen.com • www.dressedonline.com
....

The two shopping districts in an affluent suburb of Santa Barbara are known to locals as Upper (Montecito) and Lower (Coast Village) because they sit two miles apart. Upper's woodsy setting is where visitors grab a deli sandwich, and seek treasures at clothing and antique shops. Coast Village's huge eucalyptus trees line

a quaint country road with upscale boutiques. Maison K is a mix of fine home furnishings and gifts from around the world. Eco-conscious Living Green has been selling environmentally sound materials and children's items since 1999. Rest those weary feet and paws at Scoop's gelato parlor before heading to Dressed clothing store for Balenciaga and Yigal Azrouel designer gems.

WILLIAM LAMAN

1496 East Valley Road, Montecito, CA 93108
(805) 969-2840 • www.williamlaman.com

This is a sweet, diminutive cottage in Montecito Village shopping district. Unique furniture, classic garden appurtenances, and fine European antiquities lure customers and well-behaved pooches from room to room. Their slogan, "Not what you need, but what you want," sums up the store's bravado and offers no excuses. No one needs a clear glass bud vase fashioned after a marine urchin or a French Polychrome wedding tray table, but one look, and you'll want it. The selection is void of ubiquitous cookie cutter pieces. The owners philanthropic gesture offers a portion of the pro-

ceeds from antique pillows to Girls Inc. of Greater Santa Barbara
County.

STATE STREET

Between Victoria Street and Haley Street, Santa Barbara, CA 93101
(805) 966-9222 (Santa Barbara Conference & Visitors Bureau)
(805) 962-2098 x25 (First Thursday)
www.santabarbaramap.com • www.bluebee.com
www.santabarbaraca.com www.wendyfoster.com
ww.santabarbaradowntown.com
....

Many cities have a renovated, thriving downtown district chock full
of fashionable stores and restaurants; Santa Barbara is no exception. A mix of big-name shops and quirky one of a kind boutiques
line the beach town's main thoroughfare. National Lucky Brand
Jeans claims turf with local Wendy Foster women's emporium and
Blue Bee's empire of six distinctive locations catering to the masses.
Macy's and
Saks Fifth
Avenue
anchor the
brick-side-
walk artery.
On the first
Thursday
of each
month from
5 p.m. to 8
p.m. State
comes alive
with music,
gallery artist
receptions,

garden demonstrations, and interactive exhibits. Maps and guides
are available from the hotel concierge or are downloadable off the
Santa Barbara Downtown website.

ROOMS & GARDENS
924 State Street, Santa Barbara, CA 93101
(805) 965-2424 • www.roomsandgardens.com
....

It's the kind of store you never want to leave. Custom furniture inspired by the casual California lifestyle is the backdrop for the signature line of wicker pieces, as well as Paris Flea Market treasures and Chinese tea boxes swathed in Asian vintage textiles. A chicken coop in the back garden houses four plumed beauties who relinquish eggs every morning to owners Eric and Jami Voulgaris.

Leashed pups can visit the fowl. Upscale hotels seek R&G's decorating counsel. Partnering with actress Mary Steenburgen at the Santa Monica location has added a bohemian flair to the already impeccable good-taste the shop displays.

To err is human, to forgive canine.
– Unknown

THE OJAI VILLAGE

Within the square blocks of Ojai Avenue, Canada Street,
Matilija Street and Montgomery Street, Ojai, CA 93023
(805) 646-8126
www.ojaichamber.org • www.ci.ojai.ca.us
www.bartsbooksojai.com • www.madeinojai.com

....

Ojai encompasses 4.2 square miles. The village sits in the core of
downtown. This small municipality of 8,000 residents has an abundance of artists, musicians, and New Age healers who display their
works in shops along the city blocks. Leashed pets are welcome
at most establishments. Bart's Books is an outdoor bookstore with
over 100,000 new, used, and rare editions resting on shelves among
tree-shaded patios. Awnings protect the volumes from the rain.
They can be purchased on the honor system via a drop slot. Made
in Ojai sells a large array of the local's paintings, jewelry, books,
and CD's.

Veterinarian

CARE HOSPITAL (California Animal Referral and Emergency)
301 East Haley Street, Santa Barbara, CA 93101
(805) 899-CARE (2273) • www.carehospital.org

....

OJAI PET HOSPITAL
1120 Maricopa Highway, Ojai, CA 93023
(805) 646-5555 • www.ojaipet.com
Open Monday through Friday 8 a.m. to 6 p.m.
Saturday 8 a.m. to 12 noon

....

VENTURA PET EMERGENCY CLINIC
2301 South Victoria Avenue, Ventura, CA 93003
(805) 642-8562 • www.petemergencyclinic.com
Open Monday through Friday 6 p.m. to 8 a.m.
Saturday and Sunday 24 hours

....

PHOTO CREDITS:

San Diego
7 & 8 Grand Del Mar, 9 Terri Clicks, 12 W Hotel, 13 & 14 Omni Hotel, 15 & 16 The Keating, 17 The US Grant, 18 Maggie Espinosa, 19 Sheraton La Jolla, 20 & 21 Manchester Grand Hyatt, 22 The Sofia Hotel, 24 The Westin Gaslamp Quarter, 25 Hotel Solamar, 28 Tower23, 29 Hard Rock Hotel San Diego, 31 Karl Strauss Brewery, 33 Mille Fleurs, 34 Maggie Espinosa, 37 The Geisel Library, US San Diego. All Rights Reserved, 42 Oak Mountain Winery, 43 Snug Pet Resort, 46 Muttropolis.

Palm Springs
49 Viceroy Palm Springs, 50 La Quinta Resort & Club, 53 Parker Palm Springs, 54 The Westin Mission Hills Resort & Spa, 55 Hyatt Grand Champions Resort, Villas and Spa, 56 & 57 Riviera Resort & Spa, 58 Rancho Las Palmas Resort & Spa, 59 Copley's on Palm Canyon, 60 Spencer's Restaurant, 61 Le Vallauris, 65 Palm Springs Convention and Visitors Bureau, 67 City of Palm Desert.

Orange County
69 & 70 Ritz-Carlton- Mark Wieland & Ron Starr, 71 Maggie Espinosa, 72 Casa Laguna Inn & Spa, 73 Seven4One, 74 & 75 Montage Laguna Beach, 76 Surf & Sand Resort, 77 Sapphire Laguna Restaurant and Pantry, 80 Laguna Culinary Arts, 81 City of San Juan Capistrano, 82 City of Dana Point, 83 Laguna Beach Convention & Visitors Bureau, 89 The Balboa Bay Club & Resort, 90 Island Hotel Newport Beach, 91 Newport Beach Conference & Visitors Bureau, 92 Fairmont Newport Beach, 93 Costa Mesa Conference & Visitors Bureau, 94 Westin South Coast Plaza, 95 Hilton Waterfront Beach Resort, 96 Joie De Vivre Properties, 98 Basilic Restaurant, 101 Park Bench Café, 102 Balboa Bay Club & Resort, 103 Newport Beach Conference & Visitors Bureau, 104 Huntington Beach Marketing and Visitors Bureau, 105 Corey Brixen, 106 Huntington Beach Marketing and Visitors Bureau.

Los Angeles
111 Westin Long Beach, 112 Joie De Vivre Properties- Matthew Millman, 113 The Varden Hotel, 114 & 115 Terranea Resort, 116 Ritz-Carlton Marina Del Rey, 117, 119 & 122 Long Beach Convention & Visitors Bureau, 124 Plantation, 127 Loews Santa Monica, 128 Sheraton Delfina, 129 Fairmont Miramar Hotel & Bungalows, 132 & 133 Viceroy Santa Monica, 134 Hotel Casa Del Mar, 135 Shutters On The Beach, 139 Santa Monica Convention & Visitors Bureau-R. Landau, 140 Santa Monica Convention & Visitors Bureau-Sandra Stocker, 141 Jonathan Adler, 142 Santa Monica Convention & Visitors Bureau, 144 Healthy Spot, 147 The Peninsula Beverly Hills, 148 Beverly Hills Hotel & Bungalows, 150, 151 & 152 SLS Hotel, 153 Avalon Hotel, 155, 158 & 159 Beverly Hills Conference & Visitors Bureau, 162 Visit West Hollywood, 164 Palihouse Holloway Hotel, 165 & 166 Andaz West Hollywood, 167 The London West Hollywood, 168 Le Montrose Suite Hotel, 170 & 171 Visit West Hollywood, 176 L.A. Inc. Los Angeles Convention & Visitors Bureau, 177 & 178 Visit West Hollywood, 180 The Langham Huntington Hotel & Spa.

Santa Barbara
187 Santa Barbara Convention & Visitors Bureau-Jim Corwin, 188 San Ysidro Ranch, 190 Four Seasons Resort The Biltmore, 191 Canary Hotel, 192 & 193 Ojai Valley Inn and Spa, 198 Santa Barbara Convention & Visitors Bureau-J. Sinclair, 200 & 201 Ojai Valley Chamber of Commerce, 202 Santa Barbara Convention & Visitors Bureau.